Sue Suhling

STILL WATERS

Dedicated with love
to "The Originals":

My parents, Jack and Shirley Henderson,
and my siblings,
John Henderson and Sara Kelley;

You are the primary circle of family
out of which have blossomed
grace and faith.

JANE RUBIETTA has a degree in marketing and management from Indiana University and has worked toward her Master's at Trinity Divinity School.

Jane's passion for soul restoration began at the bottom of a downward spiral into depression. "I lost myself trying to fulfill everyone's expectations of me. I lost sight of who God wanted me to become." She began to realize that her spiritual self-care was her own responsibility.

Jane's articles about sane soul care and restoration have appeared in *Today's Christian Woman*, *Virtue*, *Marriage Partnership*, *Decision*, *Christian Reader*, and *Christianity Today*. Her first book, *Quiet Places: A Woman's Guide to Personal Retreat*, was released by Bethany House Publishers in 1997. Jane's husband, Rich, is a pastor, music producer, and free-lance musician. They have three children and make their home near waters of rest in Grayslake, Illinois.

Acknowledgments

With gratitude and tremendous love, I thank God for:

My brother, John Henderson, and friends Mark Leahy, John Binder, and Mike Clark, who for years have kluged my ancient computer pieces into a functioning unit, allowing me to keep working on a tightwad's budget;

Sandra Fricke, for making it possible for the Rubiettas to have a home, thus providing daily renewal beside still waters and green pastures;

My local library: you have found, held, renewed, and located again innumerable books, obscure quotes, tedious facts, and copyright information;

Lin Johnson of WordPro Communications and Write-to-Publish Writers' Conference, for her vision to equip and empower Wanna-be Writers to become World Changers;

The godly team of publishers, publicists, and editors at Bethany House Publishers: I couldn't be in better hands;

My husband, Rich, for patiently encouraging me to find rest and restoration, and our children, Ruthie, Zak, and Josh, who remind me that part of growing up is learning how to play. Your love, even while rubbing against my rough edges and polishing me, challenges me to be more like my Shepherd.

Contents

The Lord is my shepherd;
I shall not want.
He makes me to lie down in green pastures;
He leads me beside the still waters.
He restores my soul;
He leads me in the paths of righteousness
For His name's sake. . . .
Surely goodness and mercy shall follow me
All the days of my life;
And I will dwell in the house of the Lord
Forever.

Psalm 23:1–3, 6 NKJV

Preface

Water laps at the edge of the hill, a quiet invitation. But I am busy meeting deadlines, planning a family celebration, answering the phone. When my husband, Rich, edges into my office, I dig around for a message I scrawled for him. He grins at the total dishevelment of my desk, the piles of papers and opened books and scattered pens.

"Looks like the desk of a busy writer." His voice is warm with affection and gentle tolerance.

"A busy, sloppy, tired writer," I grunt. Fatigue displays itself in my tone, my posture, and the purple shadows under my once-green, now red eyes.

He rubs my shoulders with strong hands. "Let's take the rowboat out for a short spin, Hon." His invitation tempts me, but the deadlines . . .

"What's the title of your book, Jane?" He breaks into a lopsided smile, knowing full well the title is *Still Waters: Finding the Place Where God Restores Your Soul.*

I hit F10 on the computer, saving my work, and we head down the hill. Halfway to the water, the sun on the warm green grass overcomes me. I pull Rich down, and we stretch out side by side, holding hands, letting the sunshine mend the rawness of too much busyness and too little time together. "He makes me lie down in green pastures," David said in Psalm 23, and lying there faceup, I understand why.

We will never be without work to do, and God certainly knows this. The biggest challenge of our lives, as women of the new millennium, is knowing when to quit working at the multiple tasks and roles in our lives and when to give ourselves permission to let God lead us beside still waters. The reality hurts: We cannot possibly grow in our roles unless we grow in our souls.

Still waters imply peace, and rest, and quiet. Whatever our personality type, renewal and restoration are found in stillness, in the cessation of work and the trust that must accompany that stillness. The very fact that the Shepherd leads us—by the example of Jesus, who frequently sought out solitude and silence—reminds us that we can do nothing on our own. He becomes our Shepherd when we follow Him into these places of stillness. He leads, but the choice to follow is always ours.

Still waters are essential if we are to address the issues that hinder us in our relationships, that prevent us from growing up even as we grow older—issues we'll encounter in *Still Waters*. In the suspended stillness, we are free to examine in safety, and find healing for, soul hunger, weariness, anxiety, abandonment, and depression. In solitude we receive permission and grace to face our anger, control issues, and the grasp of money on our lives. Happiness, creativity, and hospitality begin in this hushed sanctuary.

When we allow God to lead us beside still waters, much as I allowed Rich to take my hand and then row me around the lake, the greatest longing of our soul is fulfilled as our love affair with God takes over our lives.

Introduction: How to Use This Book

Still Waters, with its unique format, provides a variety of ways to spend time with God. As we seek the places where God restores our soul, this book can be used on an individual basis or in a group setting. *Still Waters* guides us in times of personal solitude, whether we steal a few minutes away from busy schedules, or get away to a retreat center to focus for longer periods on these soul issues.

In a group setting, *Still Waters* is ideal for Sunday school classes, weekly Bible studies, or even group retreats. Various components enflesh the chapter subjects and ease the anxiety of figuring out how to spend time with God. God restores our soul, bringing rest and renewal when seeking those still waters through each of the following:

- Reading for Reflection
- Quotes for Contemplation
- Scriptures for Meditation
- Journaling
- Prayers of Confession, Praise, Petition
- Moments for Creation
- Silence
- Questions for Reflection
- Hymn of Praise

Reading for Reflection

Each chapter opens with a look at a specific soul issue, examining the implications and intricacies of subjects that impact our lives and delay our growth. Limited space allows only a brief study. Thus, the reading for reflection is intended simply to introduce the subject and begin a lifelong journey of exploration for each of us.

Quotes for Contemplation

Not long after heading into the world on my own, I realized how much I needed companions on the inner voyage to maturity. The book of Hebrews speaks of the great cloud of witnesses (11:1); I longed for some of them to materialize and tell me what to do. Through the people in the Scriptures, and writings by saints who detailed their journeys, our own progress is hastened. Just as infants walk sooner when a hand guides them, so we grow with the help of the hand offered down through the ages. This section of quotes is that hand, reflecting the wisdom and experience of others intent on following hard after God. In a world lacking mentors, these people become guideposts pointing us toward maturity in Christ.

Scriptures for Meditation

God's Word is the Checkpoint Charlie for our souls. In Scripture, all the reading and journaling and soul-searching is either validated or proven false. For real growth to occur, we need to immerse ourselves in the Word of God, letting Scripture fill the shadows in our souls, inform our minds, and direct our steps.

Each passage of Scripture reflects the subject of the chapter, reminding us that God does still speak audibly to us today. Take time to soak up the Word, reading it aloud, slowly, phrase by phrase. Listen for the Holy Spirit to highlight a phrase or emphasize a passage for your instruction. Invite God to illumine your path through quiet meditation on His Word. Real restoration and healing are found in the still waters of Scripture.

Journaling

For centuries, saints have journaled to demonstrate their struggles and God's abounding love, power, and presence in their lives. The Psalms, Jeremiah, Lamentations, and other portions of Scripture read like journals, reminding us of the truth of Proverbs 14:8: "The wisdom of the prudent is to give thought to their ways" (NIV). Journaling frees us to reflect on our own lives, our interactions with others, and God's work.

Styles and types of journals abound: from clothbound books to spiral notebooks; from gratitude starters to daily prayer journals. No rules exist for journaling except honesty and openness. For the purpose of our growth, in *Still Waters* the journal provides a place for soul-searching, a safety valve for spilling toxic emotions, a record of praying with a pen, and a memento of God's whispers to our souls. The journal, then, becomes an accountability partner, revealing patterns and problems, areas of growth and God's grace. Keeping track of the state of that obscure, internal region of the spirit grants God the freedom to move us forward, growing us up into the image and likeness of the Son.

Prayers of Confession, Praise, Petition

Spiritually speaking, we frequently leapfrog into an arm's-length prayer list, jumping over the necessary elements of confession and praise. But the Scriptures remind us that if we harbor sin in our hearts, the Lord cannot answer our petitions.

> Behold, the Lord's hand is not so short that it cannot save; neither is His ear so dull that it cannot hear. But your iniquities have made a separation between you and your God, and your sins have hidden His face from you, so that He does not hear. (Isa. 59:1–2)

After journaling, confession naturally follows. God delights to pour forgiveness into that hollowness created by confession, generating a spilling of praise. How easy, then, to lay our petitions at the throne of God, knowing our gracious Lord's promise: "If you ask for a fish, God will not give you a stone, will He?"

Moments for Creation

An element too often overlooked in the pursuit of the still waters of restoration is time spent admiring the handiwork of God. "The heavens declare the glory of God," but I get caught up in the treadmill of life and forget to stop and watch. Daily, now, I try to show up at the picture window in our family room as the Creator brings up the curtain on a new day. When the sun splashes silver lamé over the water, my heart brightens with love for God.

Including time in our spiritual lives to be aware of the work of God in nature waters our parched souls and reminds us that God created beauty for two reasons: (1) As a creative God, He loves beauty, and (2) He loves us.

Silence

Henri Nouwen defined discipline as "the effort to create some space in which God can act. Discipline means to prevent everything in your life from being filled up. It means somewhere you're not occupied, and you're certainly not preoccupied. It means to create that space in which something can happen that you hadn't planned on or counted on."[1]

With silence we create a space for God to act, speak, and love. We shove aside words, both external and internal; present ourselves to God, loving Him with all our hearts; and wait. Whether we hear direct words from God, or He simply enfolds us with His loving presence, He receives our gift and our sacrifice. For silence requires trust, and a laying down of our own need to justify ourselves by words and rationalizations. The gift of silence demonstrates our willingness to trust God, to give up trying to earn His unearnable love, to rest in the work Christ has already done for us.

Sometimes silence lasts in the busy, word-rushed confines of my mind only for a few seconds. But in that silence, I find that I am energized, my day prioritized, my love for God and others revitalized by the simple act of paying attention, finally, to God.

Questions for Reflection

In my own life, I occasionally need someone to pin me to the wall, like an insect, for observation. I need people to ask hard questions about motivation and meaning and feelings, about my take on various issues and the state of my soul. This section provides those questions, prodding us into deeper waters, forcing us to examine the underwater terrain of our spirits. These questions, as well, provide an application point, forcing us to do more than read for recreation and to fill our spare minutes. When we pray and think and journal through our response, we incorporate the learning that has occurred and give the Holy Spirit a chance to change us on the inside.

Hymn of Praise

At Christmas this past year, family and friends braved sub-zero temperatures to visit elderly church members and nursing homes. As our ears reddened in the transition from frigid winds to overheated dining halls, we invited these aged saints, whose lives were written in wrinkles and smiles, to join us in the familiar carols. One woman, in spite of obvious deterioration of body and mind, could sing every verse of the theology-rich songs. Hidden away in a secret place of her heart, the words and melody lived a life of their own, still capable of transforming her physical problems into opportunities for praise.

Music reaches places in our souls that are inaccessible in any other way. Studies show that music changes mood, elevates learning, increases productivity. When we learn something through melody, we learn it for life.

Music frees our spirit to embrace God in new ways, opening us to the presence of the Holy Spirit. Hymns, one of the richest traditions of Christian worship, allow God to reinforce other forms of learning, and for this reason hymns are an integral part of the restoration beside still waters. Whether you can carry a tune or sound like a wooden bell when you sing, take time to sing or read through the selected hymn(s) in each chapter, meditating and reflecting on the truths within.

Real Restoration

As is the case with any writing on a deep subject, the limited number of pages prohibits an exhaustive (and exhausting) look at any of the subjects. Entire books, series, and lives have been devoted to the understanding of many of these issues, and I humbly offer only a limited amount of insight, and many more questions, to you, my friend and fellow seeker. Each chapter is intended simply to encourage the beginnings of soul exploration on various topics, and to give each of us permission to deal honestly with subjects too often taboo and too often experienced by Christians today. Real healing begins when we acknowledge our imperfections, our struggles, our imperfect pasts. In the acknowledgment, we are set free to join the fellowship of the unashamed.

These issues are not resolved in my own life. I still battle with abandonment, at times feel besieged with worry, struggle with the emotional meaning of money, and wrestle with anger like Jacob wrestled with God. And I'm finding, as I grapple with such things in my own life, that they are interrelated. One cannot separate, for example, abandonment from worry, or money from control. They are not mutually exclusive subjects, and so the chapters build on one another.

It is an honor to be accompanied by the Lord, held and upheld by His power through areas of healing. It is doubly humbling to realize that our gracious God can take our tentative footsteps and missteps, our slow plodding on this journey of faith, and allow us to stomp out a path for others on their soul journeys.

Though I believe in this life we will continue to work out the imperfections, I am confident of this: that He who began a good work in us will bring it to completion on the day of Christ Jesus (Phil. 1:6). With joy I submit myself to the process of that completion, and with delight I share the gleanings of that process with you. May you find that God's grace is sufficient for each day, for each trial, for each issue. May the Good Shepherd gently lead you beside still waters and restore your soul.

CHAPTER ONE

Soul Hunger

Our lives are bursting at the seams, but not with God. Job said, "My gauntness rises up, and testifies against me." Here, discover how to recognize soul hunger, and learn to be filled with all the fullness of God.

Early morning darkness watched me, unblinking, through the windows. Alone at the dining room table, I attempted to appease a craving in my soul with Scripture. I identified strongly with the words from Isaiah. A voice said, "Cry out." The listener, bewildered, asked, "What shall I cry?"

A modest attempt to pursue a dream of writing had resulted in some open doors I hadn't anticipated, and I stood looking outside, unable to see even the first step. A gnawing soul malaise ate away at any contentment I might feel with a loving husband, three precious children, and everything I needed.

Clarissa Estes named the deep cry in my breast, the pain that emanated throughout my body: she called it *hambre del alma*, the song of the starved soul.[1]

I have sung that song. I have hummed the haunting melody for much of my life, unaware of my starvation, unconscious of the wafer-thin, skeletal state of my soul. The song carries a different tune at different times; has come out in the form of tears at disconcerting moments, sounded like yelling to my children's ears, felt like incapacitating exhaustion, resounded with frantic yea-saying when it should have been nay.

"What do you do to stay alive spiritually?" I had begged other women. Few seemed to understand my plea, as lost as I was in a nightmare of diapers and dust, dishes and duties. My spiritual emaciation and hunger pangs remained, buried under a more acceptable veneer, until they consumed me like tapeworm burrowing under the skin of my life.

A Society of Starved Souls

Anorexia and bulimia run rampant in our society. Hollywood throws scalpel-sculpted bodies on the screens of our mind. Weight loss is a billion-dollar business (where but in America?!) with dietary supplements, dietary experts, and diets to fit every possible compulsion and problem. Mirrors line workout worlds around the nation; gyms bulge with people wanting to become more acceptable according to the world's definition of beauty. Women average one meal a day, nibbling around the rest of their nutritional needs. We watch our cholesterol and count fat grams, somehow believing that what we see is who we are.

Who we are is a society of starved souls, spiritual anorexics hopping from one church to another, one gimmick to another, trying to find some kind of fast food for the soul in hopes of alleviating surface hunger pains. To assuage the hunger, we join committees, do more work, never realizing that without deep soul food our good works leech the marrow from our bones. Like the prodigal child, we attempt to fill ourselves with husks from the pigpen rather than the riches from the Father's table. We cram our lives with people and possessions and let others determine our priorities.

But we have it backward. The cart before the horse. Our BEING must precede our DOING if we are to grow strong in the wilderness times. As Ruth Senter writes, when we are weary and vulnerable, looking for ways to feed our souls, God's desire is clear:

> You want to know how to motivate others to do love? It isn't by doing more love so you can be their model. It's by coming close to Me, letting My love soak into you like water saturating a sponge. Others will know when you are full. When their lives touch yours, love will seep out. Then it will be My love that motivates them, not your deeds. . . . As you drink deeply of My love, you will be strengthened and renewed. Then the doing of your love will be the overflow. . . . You

must *be* my love before you can *do* my love. Perhaps it is the greater side of faith for you to say, "I love You, Lord," and not do anything.[2]

Because in the end, the wilderness is not so much about what we accomplish, but who we become.

Wilderness Time

As the sun rose on that crisp autumn morning, I hustled two children off to school and awakened our three-year-old. After slipping him into overalls, we loaded ourselves into the car to pick up tomatoes for fall canning.

En route, the words of Isaiah rolled over and over in my mind, a never-ending refrain to the question in my spirit. "Cry out." "What shall I cry?" My very calling as a writer and speaker depended on words. But in my emptiness, I had no words. Job's lament was true for me: "My gauntness rises up and testifies against me" (16:8 NIV).

A friend's statement returned: "Sounds like you're in a wilderness, Jane." Her voice was warm and understanding. "I do know this: there's sustenance in the wilderness."

"God," my heart screamed now, as the road narrowed to a gravel lane, "You fed the Israelites in the wilderness. You brought them water from a rock. You HAVE to feed me in this time. I cannot go on without sustenance."

"Comfort, O comfort My people," the Lord said.

"Comfort me," I cried back.

We rattled into the farmyard. On previous trips I had spoken only with hired men. This day, it seems significant that I met the owner for the first time.

"Sorry, we're all out of tomatoes," he said, shaking his ruddy face back and forth for emphasis. Struggling with asthma, he wheezed, "We still have some tomatoes in the back field, though, if you want to pick them yourself." The farmer jerked his head toward the area beyond the barn.

"How much would they cost?"

"They're free if you pick them."

My eyes widened. Free? FREE!

I followed the farmer's van past a score of workers picking cabbages the size of basketballs and loading them into boxes. He pulled behind the modern, aluminum-sided barn and waved me toward a field full of collapsed vines. Tomatoes gleamed like jewels from beneath the sprawling stems and leaves.

"Help yourself," he said.

"You're sure?"

The tall man nodded and climbed back into his van, and Joshua and I clambered out of the car and waded into the mass of greenery. Within minutes, one crate—about a bushel—was full.

Straightening my back, I surveyed the field. Acres of vines tumbled around me, extravagant evidence of a farmer's industrious care of his land. I remembered Ruth, gleaning in the field along with other foreigners; the Lord's provision for the stranger and alien in the land—for His own children in the desert.

Tears scalded my eyes. The promise echoed in my mind: "Sustenance in the wilderness."

"You will feed me, won't You, Lord?" I breathed deeply, my heart shouting the doxology. The words twined around my soul like the vines in the field, whispering of blessings to come.

Promises in the Wilderness

Filling

In my hunger, I search the Scriptures like Old Mother Hubbard exploring her neighbor's cupboard. My concordance has multiple listings under *filling* and *fill*. The Word promises that we will be filled with the Holy Spirit, filled with wisdom, filled with joy, with all knowledge, with comfort. "Blessed are you who hunger now, for you shall be filled" (Luke 6:21 NKJV). Interestingly, the word "filled" in this passage leans toward supplying food in abundance, from the word for "gorge." This does not sound like starvation rations or pods from the pigsty, and hope nourishes me.

Resting

The gospel of Luke opens with the statement "He has filled the hungry with good things" (1:53 NKJV). This original word, translated here as "filled," means satisfy, but digging deeper I learn that it traces its ancestry to the word "rest." This word is rarely used with verbs of motion and indicates a fixed position. This filling is somehow related to resting. God is gracious, promising filling for the hungry soul—a filling that comes not by striving but by resting.

Watching

As always, I strain my eyes for soul models when I begin to journey down an unknown path. Isaac Newton said, "If I see farther than others, it's because I stood on the shoulders of giants." So I ask, Who has walked this way before me? Reading through the Gospels, Jesus' footprints into the wilderness mark my heart, and I study the order of events.

Bracketed by Blessings

Before Jesus set foot into the devil's playground, God arranged for a powerful send-off. We know the story. Jesus' cousin, John the Baptist, whom He undoubtedly loved, baptized Jesus with great humility. What a gift to have a loved one on hand at such a significant moment. In addition, John had spent much of his life living in the wilderness, munching on questionable food and getting acquainted with the desert life and its accompanying difficulties. How comforting to begin a difficult journey with someone who knows the path and empathizes.

As a mother, I imagine sending my firstborn off into the wilderness to be tempted and tested, and my heart quells, my spirit blanches. Imagine how the Father must have grieved at what was coming for His beloved Son. As the ultimate benediction for Jesus, the Holy Spirit came upon Him, and His Father's voice poured over Him, "Thou art My beloved Son, in Thee I am well-pleased."

Wrapped in the love of His Father, the Holy Spirit, and His flesh-and-blood cousin, Jesus was then, according to Mark 1:12, immediately impelled into the wilderness. The word "impelled" means thrust, hurled, or cast: this was no gentle prodding from behind.

Mark devotes only one more verse to the wilderness theme.

> And He was in the wilderness forty days being tempted by Satan; and He was with the wild beasts, and the angels were ministering to Him. (1:13)

I can only imagine the beasts available to one in the desert; I cannot fathom the depths of the temptation Jesus endured during those forty days. I do know this: though Jesus' body grew lean from His fast, His soul feasted on and was fortified by the Word of God and the love of God. It is the only way through the desert time, of sweltering heat by day and freezing temperatures by night, of sandstorms and blinding brightness. Jesus lived out Jeremiah's experience: "Thy words were found, and I ate them, and Thy words became for me a joy and the delight of my heart" (15:16).

In the end, the devil withdrew, and with a great deal of heavenly flurry, the angels encircled Jesus and ministered to Him.

Preparing

The wilderness time kicked off Jesus' Galilean ministry, preparing Jesus for His work and His calling. The role of the Holy Spirit during this time does not escape notice: He led Jesus, propelled Jesus, and, Luke 4:1 says, filled Jesus.

The term "wilderness," as used in Scripture, often denotes a setting for preparation for a time of ministry, of fruitfulness. When the angel of the Lord said to Philip (Acts 8:26–40 NIV), "Go south to the road—the desert road—that goes down from Jerusalem to Gaza," Philip obeyed. In the wilderness, he found the Ethiopian eunuch whose soul had been prepared to hear and receive the Word of God. The church in Ethiopia credits their very existence to this eunuch's wilderness time. Faithfulness in the preparation—in the wilderness—will mean readiness to bear fruit.

Provisions for Food

The real-life desert, of course, is not without fruit. God in His wisdom created plants that have moisture in their leaves, in their roots. The wise desert traveler knows where to look for sustenance while traversing the seemingly barren sands.

It strikes me that Jesus himself, who without doubt knew the anguish of hunger and thirst after His forty-day fast, said, "I am the bread of life; he who comes to Me shall not hunger, and he who believes in Me shall never thirst" (John 6:35). When the Jewish leaders argued that God had provided literal food in the desert for their forefathers, Jesus seized the analogy and pointed to himself. He will be our sustenance, with food that money, work, achievement, or busyness cannot buy. In the wilderness, we are weaned from all other dependencies and forced to turn to the One who himself was thrust into the wilderness. We can trust Jesus in this:

"Blessed are those who hunger and thirst for righteousness, for they shall be satisfied" (Matt. 5:6).

Fullness and Feasting

As I lean on my staff in this desert, the sand so hot it feels like I'm walking on boiling water, I know that I do not journey alone. The same Holy Spirit guides me; the same Father claims me as His child and grants me His blessing. The Word of God and worship sustained Jesus during His wilderness time (Matt. 4:4, 10). I, too, am forced to feed this soul hunger with God during this desert time, to come to the end of my own resources and rely upon heaven's. I enter the wilderness, my life bursting at the seams—but not with God.

One day I will leave this wilderness time. I pray and trust that I will be filled with all the fullness of God.

If the jars of tomatoes remaining on my shelves are a witness, it will be a feast. I will invite the angels for dinner.

Quotes for Contemplation

Whether we gaze with longing into the garden or with fear and trembling into the desert, of this we can be sure—God walked there first! And when we who have sinned and despoiled the garden are challenged now to face the desert, we do not face it alone. Jesus has gone there before us to struggle with every demon that has ever plagued a human heart. Face the desert we must if we would reach the garden, but Jesus has gone there before.

—JAMES HEALY,
STARTING POINT

Those of us who walk along this road
do so reluctantly. . . .

We'd rather be more active—
planning and scurrying around.
All this is too contemplative to suit us.
Besides we don't know what to do
with piousness and prayer.

Perhaps we're afraid to have time to think,

for thoughts come unbidden.
Perhaps we're afraid to face our future
knowing our past.
Give us the courage, O God,
to hear your word
and to read our living into it.
Give us the trust to know we're forgiven,
and give us the faith
to take up our lives and walk.

—**ANN WEEMS,**
KNEELING IN JERUSALEM

If, as Herod, we fill our lives with things,
and again with things;
if we consider ourselves so unimportant
that we must fill every moment of our
lives with action,
when will we have the time
to make the long, slow journey
across the desert as did the Magi?
Or sit and watch the stars
as did the shepherds?
Or brood over the coming
of the child as did Mary?
For each one of us,
there is a desert to travel.
A star to discover.
And a being within ourselves
to bring to life.

—**AUTHOR UNKNOWN**

The point is this: I saw more clearly than ever, that the first great and primary business to which I ought to attend every day was to have my soul happy in the Lord. The first thing to be concerned about was not how much I might serve the Lord, how I might glorify the Lord; but how I might get my soul into a happy state, and how my inner man might be nourished. . . . The first thing the child of God has to do morning by morning is to obtain food for his inner man.

As the outward man is not fit for work for any length of time except if we take food, and this is one of the first things we do in the morning, so it should be with the inner man. Now what is the food for the inner man? Not prayer, *but* the word of God; *and here again not the simple reading of the word of God, so that it only passes through our minds, just as water runs through a pipe, but considering what we read, pondering over it, and applying it to our hearts.*

—GEORGE MUELLER

O God our deliverer, you led your people of old through the wilderness and brought them to the promised land. Guide now the people of your church, that, following our Savior, we may walk through the wilderness of this world toward the glory of the world to come; through Jesus Christ our Lord, who lives and reigns with you and the Holy Spirit, One God, now and forever. Amen.

—THE LUTHERAN BOOK OF WORSHIP

Scriptures for Meditation

I have treasured the words of his mouth more than my daily bread.

—JOB 23:12 NIV

"Open your mouth wide
and I will fill it.
. . . I would feed you
with the finest of wheat;
and with honey from the rock
I would satisfy you."

—PSALM 81:10, 16

And the Word became flesh, and dwelt among us, and we beheld His glory, glory as of the only begotten from the Father, full of grace and truth. . . . For of His fullness we have all received, and grace upon grace. For the Law was given through Moses; grace and truth were realized through Jesus Christ.

—JOHN 1:14, 16–17

"What injustice did your fathers find in Me, That they went far from Me

and walked after emptiness and became empty?"

—**JEREMIAH 2:5**

Your love, O Lord, reaches to the heavens,
your faithfulness to the skies.
Your righteousness is like the mighty mountains. . . .
How priceless is your unfailing love!
Both high and low among [human beings]
find refuge in the shadow of your wings.
They feast on the abundance of your house;
you give them drink from your river of delights.
For with you is the fountain of life;
in your light we see light.

—**PSALM 36:5, 7–9 NIV**

O God, Thou art my God; I shall seek Thee earnestly;
My soul thirsts for Thee, my flesh yearns for Thee,
In a dry and weary land where there is no water.
Thus I have beheld Thee in the sanctuary,
To see Thy power and Thy glory.
Because Thy lovingkindness is better than life,
My lips will praise Thee.
So I will bless Thee as long as I live;
I will lift up my hands in Thy name.
My soul is satisfied as with marrow and fatness,
And my mouth offers praises with joyful lips.

—**PSALM 63:1–5**

"Truly, truly, I say to you, it is not Moses who has given you the bread out of heaven, but it is My Father who gives you the true bread out of heaven. For the bread of God is that which comes down out of heaven, and gives life to the world. . . . I am the bread of life; he who comes to Me shall not hunger, and he who believes in Me shall never thirst."

—**JOHN 6:32–33, 35**

Journaling

The wilderness is an invitation to slow down, to contemplate, to trust that God will lead us beside still waters and restore our souls. The journal is a safe place to pour out before the Lord all the soul hunger, the longing for rest and comfort and guidance.

Prayers of Confession, Praise, Petition

Like a loving daddy, our God longs to hear everything that's on our hearts, both good and bad. Spend time confessing your sins, praising God for such unearned love, and placing your concerns in His capable hands.

Moments for Creation

Survey your surroundings for evidence of God's faithfulness. Our Lord's faithfulness doesn't depend on the circumstances at all; whether in nature or in our own lives, He is working diligently behind the scenes to ensure the outcome of these wilderness times.

Silence

Jesus is able to still the wind and the waves; He is able to still our anxious thoughts in His presence. Allow the peace and presence of God to comfort you and fill you in the desert. We thirst for an awareness of God; may He make himself known to you in the silence.

Questions for Reflection

1. When have you experienced times in the wilderness? What is the state of your soul right now? Gaunt? Full to overflowing? Somewhere in between? Share some of your deepest longings.

2. In what ways have you seen God provide still waters and rest for your soul? In what tangible ways has God demonstrated provisions for you?

3. If this is a wilderness time, what kind of send-off did you have? Who surrounds you in support, brackets you with blessings?

4. A longing to live spiritually significant lives is at the root of much of our hunger. Where do you see this in your own life?

5. The lighter we travel, the easier the trip. Is there baggage you need to discard? What has God impressed upon you during this desert time concerning your priorities, activities, busyness, and spirituality?

6. How can you best take care of your soul as you journey?

Hymn of Praise

LORD, SPEAK TO ME

Lord, speak to me, that I may speak
In living echoes of Thy tone;
As Thou has sought, so let me seek
Thy erring children, lost and lone.

O strengthen me, that while I stand
Firm on the rock and strong in Thee,
I may stretch out a loving hand
To wrestlers with the troubled sea.

O teach me, Lord, that I may teach

The precious things Thou dost impart;
And wing my words, that they may reach
The hidden depths of many a heart.

O fill me with Thy fullness, Lord,
Until my very heart o'erflow
In kindling thought and glowing word,
Thy love to tell, Thy praise to show.

O use me, Lord, use even me,
Just as Thou wilt, and when, and where;
Until Thy blessed face I see,
Thy rest, Thy joy, Thy glory share.

—**FRANCES R. HAVERGAL**

Alternate Hymn of Praise

O FOOD TO PILGRIMS GIVEN

Chorus:
Whom have I in heav'n but you?
And earth has nothing I desire besides you.
My heart and flesh may fail,
But God is the strength of my heart.
God is my portion for ever.

O food to pilgrims given,
O bread of life from heaven,
O manna from on high!
We hunger; Lord, supply us,
Nor thy delights deny us,
Whose hearts to thee draw nigh.

O stream of love past telling,
O purest fountain, welling
From out the Savior's side!
We faint with thirst; revive us,
Of thine abundance give us,
And all we need provide.

O Jesus, by thee bidden,
We here adore thee, hidden
In forms of bread and wine.
Grant when the veil is risen,
We may behold, in heaven,
Thy countenance divine.

—WORDS: TRANS. JOHN ATHELSTAN, LAURIE RILEY

Music: For alternate arrangement, listen to the companion album *Still Waters* by Rich Rubietta.

CHAPTER TWO

Let the Weary Rest

Thomas Edison invented the light bulb in 1879, and we've been burning it ever since. With fatigue a number one health concern for women, we are forced to examine the roots of our rest-less-ness. The costs of our exhaustion are far-reaching, with implications for our spiritual lives as well.

Snores sounded from the car's various occupants. The children slept soundly in their car seats and seat belts. Rich snoozed on the passenger side. Outside, a brilliant moon created stark, dramatic silhouettes of barns and silos. Because I don't sleep in cars, I designate myself the night driver. And because we determined early in parenting that it's easier to make tracks on a trip with the children sleeping (rather than complaining or fighting), we tend toward night trips.

This night, thirty miles from home, I rounded a curve and found myself in the wrong lane. I jerked the car back, away from the field on the left side of the road. Absolute terror shook me. What if there'd been a car there when I nodded off for those two seconds? What if I'd landed in that field? What if. . . ? According to the National Highway Traffic Safety Administration, upward of 1,800 deaths and 103,000 car accidents are caused by dozing drivers each year.[1]

Why do we drive without sleep? Indeed, why do we spend so much time awake and so little time in the sack? According to researchers, Americans live with a massive "sleep debt;" most of us go without the necessary eight to nine hours of sleep we need each night.

In fact, in my private poll, *Tired* ranked third in answers to the question "How are you?" coming only after responses *Fine* and *Busy*. Like the first two answers, *Tired* is almost a meaningless response, like answering "What are you?" with the word *Human*. Of course we are. Human. Busy. Tired.

Between 1.5 and 2 million Americans suffer from chronic fatigue syndrome, a disease of the immune system and brain that causes insomnia, fatigue, and other debilitating symptoms.[2] Women in the United States cited fatigue as their top-ranking health concern, even over life-threatening illnesses such as heart disease and breast cancer.[3] The top two reasons for their fatigue included the combination of home and outside work and lack of sleep. We are a perpetually fatigued people.

Costs of Fatigue

The lack of sleep reaps disturbing problems. In addition to traffic accidents and fatalities, this sleep debt drains $50 to $70 billion from our national economy each year.[4] It shows up in lowered productivity, accidents, sleepiness during daytime hours, and possibly even illness. Sleep debt may have been partially to blame in such disasters as Three Mile Island, the Exxon Valdez, and the Challenger.[5] On a more personal level, researchers found that a half-night's sleep loss causes a 50 percent reduction in the cells that scavenge the blood for infected cells. To be chronically short on sleep may be asking for trouble.[6] In fact, sleeping less than six and a half hours a night can shorten your life.[7] This slogan on a T-shirt may be more prophetic than we know: "Rest When You're Dead."

Of course, women know that lack of sleep affects health—at least the health of others. How many times have we gone on vacation and, after the great push to get caught up on work and ready to go, arrive at the destination with a sick husband? Or watching the grueling schedule of an adolescent, full of late nights of homework and early morning commitments and sports, we privately predict, "Next, she'll get sick." Three days later, our achiever complains of a scratchy throat, headache, chills.

Sleep makes sense. Still, we have millions of workers on the midnight shift, late-night TV, round-the-clock trucking schedules, megawatt lights so we can play our sports in the dark, and red-eye flights. (Now THAT'S an encouraging thought: The pilot on our red-eye is off his natural body clock just as we are!) We seem intent on fighting the darkness, on defying our body's natural limits and needs.

Besides staying well, there are other vital reasons for sleep.

Reasons for Rest

We cheat ourselves when we don't get our rest. Our families suffer for our sleep deprivation. Stanley Cohen, a neuropsychologist, says sleep debt can make you "clumsy, stupid, unhappy, and dead."[8] Such symptoms might affect our loved ones, as well as our work. In addition, creativity suffers when we choose wakefulness over sleep. Studies show that people tend to be more rigid at problem-solving after loss of sleep than when rested.[9] While I was sleepless in college, experts learned that the brain waves for creativity exactly replicate those for REM (rapid eye movement, or dream) sleep. They then conducted experiments that prohibited patients from moving into the dream stage of sleep for a sustained period. The result? Induced psychosis in those patients.

Obvious physical reasons surround the importance of sleep. The buildup of germ-killer cells, for one. For another, during sleep our bodies literally remake themselves. In one year, 98 percent of our bodies is totally new: new liver (every six weeks), new skin (every month), new stomach lining (every five days), new bones (every three months). Even lungs blackened by years of smoking are pink as a baby's seven years after quitting.

Sleep shucks off stress and its ill-effects, repairing damage done during daylight. Rest rebuilds our endocrine and cardiovascular systems. Besides that, sleep feels heavenly.

So, *why* do we live with this expensive sleep debt? Why don't we sleep?

Why the Weary Don't Rest

Many potential reasons exist for our sleepless patterns and widespread fatigue. The eighty-four sleep disorders, including insomnia, apnea, and sleepwalking, affect some of us, but most are treatable.[10] Depression and chronic pain can also interfere with sleep. (Sleeplessness is both a cause and a symptom of depression, which is discussed in chapter 4.) But what about the rest of us, rest-less for other reasons?

Friends say they hate to go to bed because "I'm afraid I'll miss something." Or, "Bedtime always seemed like a punishment when I was a child." Or, "If I go to sleep, I lose control of the people in my home who are still awake."

Physiological problems aside, we are increasingly a people driven to produce, achieve, accomplish. By our output, we attempt to quantify, and thus justify, our existence. We live in a society that values and applauds hard work, and we use hard work to feel better about ourselves. We have taken the Scripture to heart, mistakenly, which calls us to work out our salvation with fear and trembling (Phil. 2:12). Perhaps if we do enough, work enough, produce enough, we can balance the heavenly scales in our favor.

I served on a ministry team with a man who worked incessantly. We talked about his theology of ministry, and he sternly told me, "I'd rather burn out than rust out." He did. He dropped dead of a heart attack in the prime of ministry. This seems like both poor theology and poor stewardship to me.

We cannot DO enough to justify our existence; if we could, Christ's death would have been unnecessary. In no sense can we EARN our place in heaven through hard work and resultant fatigue. Our very existence is justification itself, proving our worth. If God had not deemed us worthy of living, He would not have created us in the first place. The passage in Philippians continues, "For it is God who is at work in you, both to will and to work for His good pleasure." GOD, not our good works, justifies our existence.

Why, then, the ceaseless striving? Is it so difficult to trust God and get our rest? Do we not believe the Scriptures, which admonish us of the futility of rising early and working late? (Ps. 127:2) Do we not believe that the Lord our God neither slumbers nor sleeps? (Ps. 121:4) If God is awake, need we be awake and watchful also?

A Spiritual Foundation

God created day and night for a reason. People and plants grow in the darkness. One of the reasons Alaska doesn't grow corn is because it requires nighttime for growth, and the sun gets scant shut-eye in Alaskan summers. (They do grow incredible cabbage, though.) Grow lights don't work for corn, and they don't work for people either.

We don't trust the darkness. Bad things happen in the dark, and problems always seem worse at night, in the dark, or when we're tired. All the undones, and the poorly dones, haunt us without the sun. Sleep symbolizes trust, showing an intimate connection between our personal responsibility for life and God's role. Thus, bedtime becomes a battle zone between our desire to trust God and our need to keep life under a firm grip of control. Sleep, in my soul dictionary, means *rest*.

Spiritually speaking, sleep reminds us of the limits of our humanity, of the finiteness of our condition. In the Creation account, what did the Lord do on the seventh day? Work some more? Tie up loose ends to prepare for the next week? Strive to meet another deadline? Pull out the ol' DayTimer and schedule a new project?

No. On the seventh day, God rested. The Scriptures read,

> And by the seventh day God completed His work which He had done; and He rested on the seventh day from all His work which He had done. Then God blessed the seventh day and sanctified it, because in it He rested from all His work which God had created and made. (Gen. 2:2–3)

Our Creator rested not because He was tired or His muscles ached or His circadian rhythm was off. He rested to show us a natural rhythm of work and rest, of toil and trust. Here we find the correlation between "six days you shall labor" (Ex. 20:9) and the commandment "You must deny yourselves, and do no work" (Lev. 16:29 NIV). Unlike God, we feel like we never complete anything, and so we press on. Work, so tangible, provides an obvious, instant sense of worth. To deny ourselves is to deny our natural compulsion to achieve, to earn—to trust in our own efforts.

The Israelites needed constant reminding that they could not save themselves. References to the Lord providing for their needs and for their rest appear throughout the Old Testament: rest for His people, their slaves, and the stranger in the midst, as well as for their animals (Ex. 23:11–12); rest for the land (Lev. 25:20–23); rest from war (Josh. 14:15). Resting in God was an indication of the Israelites' spiritual condition. As was their lack of rest.

So our fatigue and our incessant activities indicate our own spiritual condition. We, too, identify with the passage in Jeremiah:

> My people hath been lost sheep: their shepherds have caused them to go astray, they have turned them away on the mountains: they have gone from mountain to hill, they have forgotten their restingplace. (Jer. 50:6 KJV)

Like the Israelites of long ago, we forget that God longs to be our restingplace. To what shepherds have we listened, as we go from mountain to hill? Hollywood sounds a clarion siren call: "Imitate my rich and famous, and you will find fulfillment." Fifth Avenue pumps billions of dollars each year into marketing to convince us that THEIR products will help us feel good about ourselves. We listen to neighbors rave about their swimming pool or their riding lawn mower. We gaze with lust at the commercials promising renewed youthfulness if we buy that new car. Children shoot one another for name-brand shoes. We transfer our affections from what God offers to what money can buy and work harder and longer to be certain of attaining the next consumable. And we transfer our values to our children, saying, "trust in God," but teaching them by our lives to trust in work and what it can buy. We lead others from mountain to hill, and cause them, too, to forget that God is their restingplace.

The Secret

Women have been sold a bill of goods. We have been told we can—and should—do everything, be everything, have everything. Now we can purchase water spiked with caffeine to push us through the process. This Great American Lie destroys individuals, marriages, families, and morals. It didn't take me long to ask, "What's wrong with me?" when I couldn't hold together hearth, home, and friendships, and still work full time. We howl with Jeremiah, "We are worn out, there is no rest for us" (Lam. 5:5). We do not need an accelerated society. We need a restingplace.

There is only One.

In my office at home, I can hear my husband in his study as he composes music and sets it to Scripture. During one rest-less period, when under some self-imposed professional deadline, I simply could not sleep at night. I dreaded nighttime, and every morning I moaned while dragging myself out of bed, "I was awake most of the night again." I dressed in the rags of fatigue, exhausted in body, brain, and soul. I couldn't string words together; I forgot the names of things. And people. Like my children.

Meanwhile, from across the hall, the words "find rest, O my soul, in God alone" (Ps. 62:5 NIV) mingled with my own thoughts from John 15 about abiding in Christ. Imagining myself lying back in the arms of Jesus, I groggily made my way to our bedroom. And slept. Nap after nap, night after night, I saw myself held securely in His arms, and my pace, which was quickened by terror at not fulfilling my obligations—not working hard enough or smart enough—slowed and became deliberate.

Here, I think, is the secret to finding God as our restingplace, part of what the book of Hebrews talks about as "entering that rest." When the psalmist says of God in Psalm 23, "He leads me beside still waters," he means the lovely image "waters of rest." More and more, as we seek to live and work and sleep in Christ's presence, we experience that rest. We find those waters of rest when we seek Him in solitude and further challenge our work ethic, forcing the issue: Do I trust my own efforts and activities, or can I trust God now to keep my world spinning while I rest with Him? When we rest from our labors we begin to trust God.

Resting, for me, means placing myself in God's hands. My thoughts, loved ones, activities, emotions, efforts, my ceaseless striving—in God's hands.

Rest is also a death. A small death perhaps, but a death nonetheless. We die to ourselves when we choose to rest in God, when we place ourselves in His loving care, when we choose to surrender small chunks of precious time in order to spend them with God in solitude, in contemplation, in rest. We die to ourselves when we choose not to pummel God with more words in our feeble efforts at prayer but to simply sit with Him as with a friend in silence, trusting instead of our own words, the Spirit's words on our behalf. For even in our silence, the Holy Spirit intercedes for us, praying for us and through us.

This is the miracle: that when we are most still, God is most active. That God's purposes are best accomplished through our inactivity. That God alone is our restingplace.

Quotes for Contemplation

Most of us today run in the fast lane of life. We choose this "lane" for a myriad of reasons. We must examine the bulky weight of constant busyness, for we will have difficulty finishing our race at the speed with which some of us are running. If we're going to persevere, then we must learn to run with *rest, the comfort and refreshment that the Lord so lovingly provides. . . .*

Physical rest is very important, but in order to keep running we also need an inner *rest—the peace and refreshment that come only from the Lord. . . .*

To pace ourselves in our race, we must make it a priority to withdraw to replenish ourselves spiritually, emotionally, and physically. We cannot allow ourselves to let busyness control our lives, so that we fall down exhausted at the end of the race. That is not freedom! There is much to do in this life, but God wants us to do all that we do in His Name and to His glory. To honor that request, we must come to Him often for the inner rest, refreshment, and guidance that is needed to run our race.

—CYNTHIA HEALD,
BECOMING A WOMAN OF FREEDOM

What is "resting in God," but the instinctive movement and upward glance of the spirit to him; the confiding of all one's griefs and fears to him, and feeling strengthened, patient, hopeful in the act of doing so! It implies a willingness that he should choose for us, a conviction that the ordering of all that concerns us is safer in his hands than in our own.

—JAMES D. BURNS,
FROM THE TREASURY OF DAVID
BY CHARLES H. SPURGEON,
AS QUOTED IN BECOMING A WOMAN OF FREEDOM

Like the dove that flew from the ark and found no restingplace for the sole of her foot (Gen. 8:9), so we fly and flutter seeking solid ground and a place of rest, but we find none. We can no longer afford to live this way. Like the Israelites, we must remember that God is our restingplace forever.

—JANE RUBIETTA

Don't be unwise enough to think that we are serving God best by constant activity at the cost of headaches and broken rest. . . . We may be doing too much. We want—at least this is my own want—a higher quality of work. Our labor should be to maintain unbroken communion with our blessed Lord; then we shall have entire rest, and God abiding in us; that which we do will not be ours, but His.

—JOHN KENNETH MACKENZIE,
AS QUOTED IN BECOMING A WOMAN OF FREEDOM

Resting does not come naturally to me, nor is it reinforced in our society or our churches. Our world applauds the opposite: leadership, independence, control, hard and unceasing work. No one teaches us to rest.

Except Jesus. Jesus lived his rhythmn of work and withdrawal, solitude and service, engagement and disengagement. His rest *in the Father established the pace of His life and the peace of His calling. He went to the mountains to pray, slipped away before dawn to be with God, and modeled a life filled with resting.*

We cannot do what Jesus did *unless we* live like Jesus lived.

—**JANE RUBIETTA**

Contemplation is variously described as a "resting" in God, or a "loving gaze" upon him, or a "knowing beyond knowing," or a "rapt attention" to God. . . . To be a follower of Jesus, to be incorporated into him and to receive his Spirit, includes the potential of sharing in the contemplative experience. Indeed, in this sense it is our birthright as children of the same Father, and will become literally a "lifeline" of communication for his faith-filled follower.

—**THELMA HALL,**
TOO DEEP FOR WORDS:
REDISCOVERING LECTIO DIVINE

Scriptures for Meditation

My people hath been lost sheep: their shepherds have caused them to go astray, they have turned them away on the mountains: they have gone from mountain to hill, they have forgotten their restingplace.

—**JEREMIAH 50:6 KJV**

In vain you rise early
and stay up late,
toiling for food to eat—
for he grants sleep to those he loves.

—**PSALM 127:2 NIV**

I will lift up my eyes to the mountains;
From whence shall my help come?
My help comes from the Lord,
Who made heaven and earth.

He will not allow your foot to slip;
He who keeps you will not slumber.
Behold, He who keeps Israel
Will neither slumber nor sleep.

—**PSALM 121:1–4**

When you lie down, you will not be afraid;
When you lie down, your sleep will be sweet.

—**PROVERBS 3:24**

I will lie down and sleep in peace,
for you alone, O Lord,
make me dwell in safety.

—**PSALM 4:8 NIV**

For indeed we have had good news preached to us, just as they also; but the word they heard did not profit them, because it was not united by faith in those who heard. For we who have believed enter that rest. . . .

There remains therefore a Sabbath rest for the people of God. For the one who has entered His rest has himself also rested from his works, as God did from His.

Let us therefore be diligent to enter that rest.

—**HEBREWS 4:2–3, 9–10**

Further Scriptures for meditation include Mark 6:31 and Matthew 11:28–30.

Journaling

Consider, as you think with ink in your journal, how the way you live your life reflects your basic beliefs about work and withdrawal, toil and trust.

Prayers of Confession, Praise, Petition

In times of prayer, we invite the Holy Spirit to search our hearts, to reveal the sin hidden in our efforts or lack of efforts. Allow God to purify you during this time, that praise may bubble forth freely as you are freely forgiven. What a thrill, then, to place our loved ones and our concerns into the all-capable hands of our Beloved and find rest for our souls.

Moments for Creation

"The heavens and the earth are around us that it may be possible for us to speak of the unseen by the seen; for the outermost husk of creation has correspondence with the deepest things of the Creator," wrote George MacDonald.[11]

Let that creation speak to you as you seek the Creator in the beauty of the outdoor world.

Silence

Madame Jeanne Guyon said, "Rest. Rest. Rest in God's love. The only work you are required now to do is to give your most intense attention to His still, small voice within."

As you seek God in the silence, imagine resting in His arms, safe, secure. Let His presence in the quiet fill the crevices of your soul.

Questions for Reflection

1. How often do you awaken rested, renewed, and ready for the day? How many hours do you actually sleep each night?

2. What are some of the reasons you fight sleep or resist changing your sleep habits? How did you feel about sleep as a child?

3. In your own life, what relationship do you see between work and worth? Do you find yourself working harder to feel better about yourself?

4. When have you experienced the presence of God in the midst of your work, a sense of His working in you while you rest in Him? How can God be your restingplace in spite of heavy responsibilities? What would need to change in your schedule and priorities?

Hymn of Praise

THOU HIDDEN SOURCE OF CALM REPOSE

(to the tune of "Faith of Our Fathers")

Thou hidden source of calm repose,
thou all sufficient love divine,
my help and refuge from my foes,
secure I am if thou are mine;
and lo! from sin and grief and shame
I hide me, Jesus, in thy name.

Thy mighty name salvation is,
and keeps my happy soul above;
comfort it brings, and power and peace,
and joy and everlasting love;
to me with thy dear name are given
pardon and holiness and heaven.

Jesus, my all in all thou art,
my rest in toil, my ease in pain,
the healing of my broken heart,
in war my peace, in loss my gain,
my smile beneath the tyrant's frown,
in shame my glory and my crown.

In want my plentiful supply,
in weakness my almighty power,
in bonds my perfect liberty,

my light in Satan's darkest hour,
in grief my joy unspeakable,
my life in death, my heaven in hell.

—**Charles Wesley**

CHAPTER THREE

Abandoned to God

Few of us were left on a doorstep as infants, and yet many of us protect ourselves in relationships as if we're afraid of abandonment or rejection. What are the roots of this fear, and how do we find safety in our relationships?

The road narrowed and the hills rose, a sure sign we were nearing the little cabin in the woods of Michigan's Upper Peninsula. Anticipation and more than a little confinement fever edged our voices. I topped a hill, Rich in the passenger seat and the children strapped in the back. Looking toward oncoming traffic, I pointed to the left side of the road. "What's that? A pile of dirt?" As we drew nearer, I gasped. "It's a bear! It's been hit!"

"Turn around," Rich said. "Let's get closer." He checked out the bear, then gave the kids clearance to see. My own face in the rearview mirror grew pale and strained. My heart thudded. Other cars stopped, turned around, drivers gawking, crowd gathering. Even in the Upper Peninsula, where bears thunder through the woods carefree and unrestrained, a bear stretched across the roadside was unusual. The shaking inside did not quell, so I, too, got out of the car.

Some vehicle had struck the bear in the hip. A big bullet hole, no doubt to put her out of her pain, pierced her furry chest. Her teats, exposed to the world, revealed that she was a nursing mamma. The vulnerability of that pink flesh surrounded by dark, coarse fur hurt me. In directing traffic for her cubs, she got them across the highway but gave up her life in the end.

The image of the cubs confused in the woods on the opposite side of the road gripped me. When the horror of abandonment, of senseless death, blurred my eyes with tears and I felt the sobs rising in my throat, I knew it was time to leave. Blinking away the wetness, I pulled my own cubs from the death scene and into the car, containing my emotions until I could examine them without traumatizing the children.

Abandonment and Fear of Intimacy

Throughout college I flitted from relationship to relationship, dating broadly and usually briefly. Once, when I was home on a visit without a guy in tow, my mother asked where my most recent beau had gone. I shrugged. She inquired insightfully, "What are you afraid of, Jane?"

Her question found its target. I had left a relationship I valued on the roadside because I was afraid.

The bear incident tapped into the fear I have of being in a relationship. "To be deserted by love," writes Ruth Senter, "is quite possibly the worst torture of the soul."[1] I don't want to invest because I don't want to be like the cubs who were left alone with no one to teach them to hunt, to fish, to save their lives. This fear of abandonment plays itself out in my life. Close relationships frighten me. I hesitate to get wrapped up in my marriage because it might not be a lifelong commitment. And in our flimsy tenements—these flesh-and-blood buildings—we have no permanence, no truly sheltering relationships that can endure, so I don't invest there either. I become a relational miser, not trusting any bank or certificate of deposit or mutual fund because of the risk involved. I hoard my relationship skills and needs and bury them for safekeeping in a mattress or a field.

No one issues guarantees; there is no Federal Deposit Insurance Corporation for relationships.

Examining this fear of abandonment, I realize that it is twofold. I don't want to invest in relationships because I fear others will fail me. But I also hold myself back because I'm afraid I'll fail; that I won't be able, as the country song goes, to "love without end, amen"; that I won't be able to merit that kind of commitment from others. I fear losing love because I don't measure up.

And so, in craving safety, solitude becomes the only place where I am safe: protected from relationships, pain, judgment, and misunderstandings. My journal always understands me, my computer is totally nonjudgmental, and thus in solitude I am actually free of commitments and responsibility, of others' expectations and needs.

No wonder I'm a hermit having a love affair with words: writing meshes perfectly with my own fears and personality defects.

Understanding the Fear of Abandonment

Whether we avoid commitments or fling ourselves into unsafe relationships, this longing for permanence and safety pervades our society today. The Scriptures point out, "What a man desires is unfailing love" (Prov. 19:22 NIV). Perhaps that explains the soaring popularity of romance novels, with an estimated forty-five million North American readers.[2] Because our desire is for permanent love, fear of abandonment lies at the core of many of our issues and may show up as physical, emotional, or spiritual abandonment in our lives.

Physical Abandonment

Diane's father died when she was three. For months she cried through the night, insisting on a light. Her father's death impacted her deeply, and when she married, Diane saw how this fear muzzled her family. If her husband was one minute late coming home from work, she fretted that he'd died in an accident. As her children grew, Diane loosened her hold on them, but panic still gripped her heart. What if they walked away and never came back? What if their relationship changed permanently?

Emotional Abandonment

Whether our fear originates with death, desertion, divorce, or another loss, we live in a world of broken commitments, broken love. We all experience emotional abandonment at some point in our lives. Most of us can relate to David's wail, "I looked for sympathy, but there was none, and for comforters, but I found none" (Ps. 69:20 NIV). Children of divorce drag their fears into nonmarriages, choosing the noncommitment of living together rather than risking marriage and divorce.

Young students carry their emotional abandonment to the classroom. So Sarah, a teacher, tries not to be absent, because children need consistency. Once, when she returned from a sick day, little George took one look at her and turned his back. "You weren't here," he accused. He wouldn't talk to her all day.

This fear of abandonment may be subtle: a withdrawing, an unwillingness to be open, a lack of spontaneous sharing, laughter, and touching. It may keep us from resolving conflict, asking hard questions, setting limits on our children, establishing boundaries. Or we may impose impossible standards on ourselves and others. "If you love me, prove it," we demand, and they can't prove it, because no one can. This fear shows itself in refusal to trust: If we don't trust, we won't be disappointed by people. Such a basic feeling of insecurity believes "If I'm abandoned, then I'm really not valuable or important." It's easy, then, to invest in tangibles, to get caught up in surface living, focusing on material things, the "hardware" of living, rather than the "heartware."

Our abandonment fear can choke our relationships: excessively controlling others, taking someone's lateness or change in plans personally, demanding 100 percent accountability for another's time. We make choices that perpetuate our abandonment fears. As the twelve-step group states,

> We either become alcoholics, marry them, or both, or find another compulsive personality to fulfill our sick abandonment needs. . . . We are dependent personalities who are terrified of abandonment and will do anything to hold on to a relationship in order not to experience painful abandonment feelings which we received from living with sick people who were never there emotionally for us.[3]

Abandonment fears keep us from exploring other aspects of the word *abandonment*. What does it mean to dance with abandon like King David before the Lord? To abandon all self-consciousness? To lose oneself in an act or emotion? This is a different way of looking at abandonment. And, rather than being the flip side of the fear of abandonment, this is probably the outgrowth of it: the need to be rigidly in control of any pleasure-producing possibilities, whether sensual—seeing, hearing, touching, smelling, tasting; or emotional—praising, laughing, loving, feeling. Fear of abandonment keeps us from acting, from loving, with abandon.

Spiritual Abandonment

With emotional and physical abandonment issues operating in us subconsciously, it's no surprise that we often bring our sense of abandonment into our relationship—or nonrelationship—with God. After all, how can we trust a God we can't see? If a mother or father, whom we can see, could forsake us, how can we trust some intangible spirit being?

Then, too, at times we trust God but have no sense of His presence. This may look like unanswered prayer or silence on God's part; in this state, suffering may be perceived as punishment. The psalmist cries, "How long, O Lord? Will you forget me forever? How long will you hide your face from me?" (Ps. 13:1 NIV).

In his book *Prayer: Finding the Heart's True Home*,[4] Richard Foster suggests that being faced with God's hiddenness can be expected, even embraced, as part of the prayer experience. That these times of darkness, when God seems removed from us, do not indicate that He is displeased with us, or that we have sinned horrifically. This sense of God's absence may in fact be grace disguised, because we are forced to change our own idolatrous image of God. Times of seeming spiritual abandonment thus become places of grace.

Through that very act of weaning us of our idolatrous images of himself, God offers us a chance to heal. Whether our issues are physical, emotional, or spiritual abandonment, we cannot live abundantly in a state of withdrawal, refusing to connect.

Overcoming Abandonment Fears

Hospitalized with a high-risk pregnancy, Libby realized that her mother would never be an emotional or practical support to her. She had not offered to care for the children left at home, to help with meals, even to visit her only child in the hospital. "I'm sick of griping about it," Libby said. "It only makes me more frustrated and angry." Instead, she chose to follow several steps for healing.

Be realistic. Whenever she began to feel depressed or angry over her mother's absence, Libby reminded herself, "My mother will never change. I cannot look to her for support."

Be real. This includes being honest about her feelings. Libby devoted time to the grief process, conceding her loss of a real mother and giving herself time and permission to cry.

Redirect. Libby asked herself, "In what relationships do I feel safe? Where have I found people who nurture me as a mother would? Where do I see God's provision for mother models, for surrogate family?"

As we ourselves choose to be realistic, to be real, and to redirect our search for safe relationships, we learn to change our focus from earthly disappointments to eternal actions.

Focus on the Present

On that summer vacation in Michigan, Rich and I took turns as caregivers and cooks, giving blocks of time to the other for solitude and reflection. I took my rummage sale sleeping bag into the woods and built a fire, the image of the cubs alone in the forest freshly imprinted on my mind. I fell in love with a frog, croaking his throaty, barreled song. Sunlight dappled and waved; mosquitoes buzzed with the frequency of a Luftwaffe air raid.

I stretched out on the sleeping bag and stared through the porthole in the wall of pine branches. Blue sky waited patiently for the drifting clouds to pass, and I waited in God's presence. I got the distinct impression He was directing me to look for His love in the present moment: in the speckled fawn camouflaged in dappled light, in the person I meet, the child I push on the swing, a fistful of daisies from a grinning, dark-eyed son.

Some call this the sacrament of the present moment. Even in the pain, the change, the uncertainty of life, we can find God's love. Living in the present forces us to move beyond the pain of past abandonment and any fear of future desertion. By focusing on "loving the one we're with," we find God's presence, and there, we feel no fear of the future. Because even though no mortal relationship ensures perfect love, in God we finally find someone who issues guarantees. Because God's "perfect love casts out fear" (1 John 4:18). To find that guarantee, we have to focus on God's work in the past.

Focus on the Past

In the still, dark sanctuary on Good Friday, two men begin the hammering blows. My soul cringes; wracking sobs convulse me. The psalmist's cry echoes through dark corridors of time, bouncing off frowning skies pierced by a cross.

"My God, My God, why have you forsaken me?" Jesus' words hit me like a stun gun. My sin, my lack of faith, separate me now from God and pinned Jesus on that cross. And there, on the cross, Jesus guaranteed what we could not: love without fail.

In this love we know, finally, the promise for the future.

Focus on the Future

I learned quickly that the connection with humans was too fragile, too tenuous, like gossamer when I needed a bridge cable. My faith is like a two-stranded rope: one strand, from me to God, is thin as a spider's web and equally flimsy. But the other, from God to me, is a band of steel in the form of Jesus Christ.

Earthly relationships were not meant to provide permanence; people *will* disappoint us. But our greatest desire—unfailing love—was planted in our hearts by the only One who could fulfill that need. In Christ, our adoption is permanent and irrevocable. No one can snatch us out of Jesus' or the Father's hand (John 10:27–28). We have His word on it.

"I will never, no never, no never leave you nor forsake you" (Heb. 13:5, literal translation). This is the only place in Scripture where the original language uses a triple negative for emphasis. Jesus experienced abandonment on the cross that we might *never* be abandoned or forsaken again.

I cannot get my mind around that kind of love. But I can receive it. And receiving such an unfailing, unending love, we are obligated to respond.

Our Responsibility in Light of Our Adoption

A neighborhood child appears at our door. Ancient, dark, haunted eyes in a ten-year-old's body, waiting for the verdict: will I be accepted?

Maria reminds me of a street child in India, always appearing at the homes where she receives emotional handouts. This, it seems, is positive: She goes like a magnet to metal to the sources who hold and nurture her.

In this child I see my own abandonment. I become Maria, a wraith, an immigrant, different, alien, orphaned, unloved. I am meant to embrace her, to welcome her as I would welcome any child, as I would welcome Jesus. In welcoming her, I begin to heal. The discarded pieces in me reassemble and begin to mend.

Our love is to approximate the love of God in Christ Jesus. Everlasting—without respect to time; undying; through and despite our times of sin and alienation. Without or with Jesus Christ, He loves us. It is amazing, sobering, humbling, uplifting, informing, enlightening, and finally, empowering.

There will always be a Maria to remind us. Of our own sense of being orphaned, and of our own need to love. To grow in love.

Such everlasting love changes and ever challenges us. Choosing to trust in God's unfailing love (Ps. 13:5), we move out of that safety into relationships.

We step out in faith. We love. Not because we love perfectly, not because our love will be perfectly returned, but because He first loved us, perfectly, in Christ Jesus. (1 John 4:19)

Quotes for Contemplation

Gracious God,
make me sensitive to all
the evidences of your goodness;
and may I, trusting in you,
free myself of the terror of death,
and feel free to live intensely and happily
the life you have given me. Amen.

—**RUBEM ALVES**

God, of your goodness give me yourself;
for you are sufficient for me.
I cannot properly ask anything less,
to be worthy of you.
If I were to ask less, I should always be in want.
In you alone do I have all. Amen.

—**JULIAN OF NORWICH, ENGLAND**

There remains within us a love that can be awakened by the sheer grace of his love's desire for us, if we fully accept it. *Yet . . . we find this incredibly difficult. Perhaps this is why the observation has been made that most of us seem to assume that union with God is attained by laboriously ascending a ladder of virtues, which finally fashion our holiness and make us fit for him. In truth, the reverse is far more accurate: the great saints and mystics have been those who fully accepted* God's *love for* them. *It is this which makes everything else possible. Our incredulity in the face of God's immense love, and also [our] self-hate or an unyielding sense of guilt, can be formidable obstacles to God's love, and are often subtle and unrecognized forms of pride, in putting our "bad" above his mercy.*

—**THELMA HALL, R.C.,**
TOO DEEP FOR WORDS

Somehow the greatest fear of abandonment, the ultimate in desertion, is death, and Christ has taken away that place of forsakenness, of annihilation. For what we fear most, our own ceasing to be, our own nothingness, becomes a place of total embrace by the One who defied death for us.

—JANE RUBIETTA

God is always at home. It is we who have gone out for a walk.

—MEISTER ECKHART

Every man God has used first suffered adversity and seeming abandonment. Think of Jacob, running from Esau's death threats; Joseph, sold into slavery and unjustly imprisoned; Moses, fleeing Pharaoh's palace to tend sheep for 40 years; or King David, hiding from Saul's jealous rages. Yahweh deals with our pride and our self-sufficiency through adversity. . . . In adversity our intellectual knowledge becomes actual knowledge.

—LYNN N. AUSTIN,
MY FATHER'S GOD

Attachment, or bondedness, is our deepest need. This is because it is also the deepest part of the character of God. . . . Repairing bonding deficits involves two factors. First, it requires finding safe, warm relationships in which emotional needs will be accepted and loved, not criticized and judged. . . . *Second,* repair requires taking risks with our needs. *It means bringing our loneliness and abandoned feelings to other believers in the same way Jesus revealed in the Beatitudes: "Blessed are the poor in spirit, for theirs is the kingdom of heaven. Blessed are those who mourn, for they shall be comforted" (Matthew 5:3–4* NASB).

These are genuine risks. No matter how safe others appear, God allows each of us a choice to be unloving. Yet when those unattached parts of the self become connected to others, our ability to tolerate loss of love from others increases. The more we internalize, the less we need the world to approve of us constantly. This is a hallmark of maturity. Loved people can feel loved even when their circumstances are emotionally dry. This is the position of being rooted and grounded in love.

—DR. JOHN TOWNSEND,
HIDING FROM LOVE

Scriptures for Meditation

For this reason, I bow my knees before the Father . . . so that Christ may dwell in your hearts through faith; and that you, being rooted and grounded in love, may be able to comprehend with all the saints what is the breadth and length and height and depth, and to know the love of Christ which surpasses knowledge, that you may be filled up to all the fullness of God.

—EPHESIANS 3:14, 17–19

How priceless is your unfailing love!

—PSALM 36:7

I have loved you with an everlasting love, therefore I have drawn you with lovingkindness.

—JEREMIAH 31:3

Can a woman forget her nursing child,
And have no compassion on the son of her womb?
Even these may forget, but I will not forget you.
Behold, I have inscribed you on the palms of My hands.

—ISAIAH 49:15–16

O Israel, put your hope in the Lord,
for with the Lord is unfailing love
and with him is full redemption.

—PSALM 130:7–8 NIV

The Lord himself goes before you and will be with you; he will never leave you nor forsake you. Do not be afraid; do not be discouraged.

—DEUTERONOMY 11:8 NIV

Do not hide Thy face from me,
Do not turn Thy servant away in anger;
Thou hast been my help;
Do not abandon me nor forsake me,
O God of my salvation!
For my father and my mother have forsaken me,

But the Lord will take me up.

—**PSALM 27:9–10**

Having loved His own who were in the world, He loved them to the end.

—**JOHN 13:1**

Journaling

As you consider your own abandonment issues, are there times when you have felt God's presence envelop you, safely and securely? Use the journal as a tool to free your thoughts and emotions, doubts and fears.

Prayers of Confession, Praise, Petition

Pour out your soul: the questions, the fears, the ugliness, the failure. Receive the forgiveness of Christ, and invite God to revamp the programming within you so that you might move into relationships without fear.

Moments for Creation

As you take time to stretch your limbs in the Lord's creation, say with the psalmist,

I'm sure now I'll see God's goodness
in the exuberant earth!
Stay with God!
Take heart. Don't quit.
I'll say it again:
Stay with God.

—**PSALM 27:13–14 THE MESSAGE**

Silence

After meditating on the Scriptures, let the words of God sink deeply into your soul. Wait for the Lord to highlight His Word for you. Worship Him in the stillness. Let Him be present with you and hold you in the silence.

Questions for Reflection

1. What memories or feelings does the subject of abandonment raise for you? Either as an adult or as a child?

2. How does the fear of abandonment impact your own relationships with loved ones? Co-workers? People at church, in the neighborhood? What are some of the primary ways this fear shows itself in your life?

3. When have you felt abandoned by God? Were you able to move back into His presence, or has the experience kept you separated? What did you do about it? When have you felt God's presence in your life today? In the past?

4. What makes you feel safe in a relationship? How can you relinquish your fears and move into your relationships more freely?

Hymn of Praise

HOW FIRM A FOUNDATION

How firm a foundation, ye saints of the Lord,
is laid for your faith in his excellent word!
What more can he say than to you he hath said,
to you who for refuge to Jesus have fled?

"Fear not, I am with thee, O be not dismayed,
for I am thy God and will still give thee aid;
I'll strengthen and help thee, and cause thee to stand
upheld by my righteous, omnipotent hand.

"When through the deep waters I call thee to go,

the rivers of woe shall not thee overflow;
for I will be with thee, thy troubles to bless,
and sanctify to thee thy deepest distress.

"When through fiery trials thy pathways shall lie,
my grace, all-sufficient, shall be thy supply;
the flame shall not hurt thee; I only design
thy dross to consume, and thy gold to refine.

"The soul that on Jesus still leans for repose,
I will not, I will not desert to its foes;
that soul, though all hell should endeavor to shake,
I'll never, no never, no never forsake."

—"K" IN RIPPON'S SELECTION OF HYMNS, 1787

CHAPTER FOUR

Into the Light: Depression

The shadows of depression affect millions of us, yet because of the social and spiritual stigma associated with this misunderstood malady, the church remains largely silent. This chapter removes the stigma, providing hope and coping strategies, and points us out of the darkness and into the light.

I feel as though I'm being submerged under water, the weight of the sea over my head; deep darkness surrounds me like a cave in the belly of the earth. I weave through corridors of darkness. No feelings exist in this cave, and I prefer it this way. I don't feel love, I don't feel joy, I don't feel sexual desire. I just want to be left alone. It's a gruesome feeling. I want to cry but no tears come. I'd love to wail but feel too self-conscious.

I don't pray to end the depression because I like not feeling. At least the negatives. I like being numb instead of angry, silent instead of ugly. I'm surprised I don't shuffle along like a lobotomy patient.

Describing the Darkness

Depression is a silent, insidious illness of body and soul that manifests itself in the mind. The quote above, excerpted from my journal, chronicles the beginning of a journey through the dark despair of depression and back into the light.[1]

This darkness can take many forms, from the blues, seasonal affective disorder (SAD), and postpartum depression, to the biochemically based, more serious bipolar (manic) and unipolar (clinical) depression. This broad spectrum can make depression difficult to diagnose, but the estimated sufferers in the United States just of the blues and SAD are ten and twenty million people, respectively.[2] Twenty-five percent of us will, at some time in our lives, experience a biochemical change in the brain that may be diagnosed as mental illness.[3] The number of people who suffer from a serious depressive episode in any given year is roughly ten million. Fewer than half of these will seek any medical treatment at all, preferring to suffer in silence rather than risk the stigma of being diagnosed with a mental illness.[4]

In spite of this, many people unfortunately do not believe that depression is a legitimate illness.

Symptoms vary. Nancy simply couldn't stop crying and couldn't figure out why she cried. Jan's depression-related panic attacks resulted in agoraphobia and chained her not only to her house but to her bed. She went from being in control to flat on her back, unable to lift her head. At work, Sandy's lowered productivity and difficulty with stress led to her quitting her job. Other common symptoms of depression include feeling sad, hopeless, or worthless; trouble sleeping or sleeping too much; difficulty concentrating and forgetfulness; unexplained low energy or fatigue; anxiety; loss of interest or pleasure; and changes in weight or appetite.

A Costly Illness

The World Health Organization predicts that depression will become the second largest global health problem within the next twenty-five years, following only heart problems in significance.[5] This is partly because people underestimate the detrimental effects depression can have on health.

Depression robs its victim of joy, of simple pleasure, of laughter, and of feelings of love. It wreaks havoc on our work and our relationships, draining our families of vitality, depriving others of our gifts of attention, service, and love. Pulling the dark cloak of depression around myself, I withdrew, wielding depression like a club to keep people away. Such isolation can contribute to the downward spiral.

The costs of depression go far beyond the personal. Depression accounts for a $43.7 billion per year burden on the American economy, measured in medical costs, lost productivity, and depression-related suicide.[6] Unfortunately, in both church and society, the widely held myths about depression keep everyone in the dark.

Myths About Depression

Christians shouldn't get depressed—if the joy of the Lord is our strength. Depression is neither a character flaw nor a sign of weak faith or unspirituality. Clinical, or endogenous, depression, like cancer or diabetes, is a physical problem with mental symptoms; externally caused (exogenous) depression results from agents outside of ourselves, such as grief, stress, or pain.

To examine this myth, I would turn to a mentor of emotions management: the king of Israel. David's life pulsates with a full spectrum of feelings. He either leaps around praising God, calls down invectives on the enemy, or begs God to lift his head, to restore the joy of his salvation.[7] The difference between David and many Christians is that he recognized and voiced his depression. The king invited God into the process of restoration, confident that with the Lord's help the depression could deepen his faith and bring him back into God's presence.

How about Elijah? The prophet's enormous spiritual and physical workout with the false priests depleted him. Depression often sweeps in after moments of significant spiritual accomplishment, as Elijah experienced after slaying the false prophets. (See 1 Kings 18–19:5 for the whole story.) We can blame the enemy—and Satan is certainly capable of taking advantage of us at such a time—but research does show a correlation between stressful (albeit victorious) situations and resultant slumps of energy and adrenaline, all of which increase the likelihood of depression.

Snap out of it! Faith's sister didn't understand Faith's depression after a messy and lengthy divorce and the fallout of helping her children cope with the changes and traumas as a single mother. Her sister's advice: "Get over it."

Mild depression is a normal response to life and loss. Failure to respect this normal response can short-circuit the healthy process of working through depression. When we honor people's time limits in dealing with this illness, we foster empathy and support, and actually encourage the depressive to continue to journey through the shadows into the light.

Depression is a pity party. Just stop focusing on yourself, and you'll be fine. Sometimes depression results from focusing on others to the exclusion of our own healthy and normal needs. Depression can become a healing process if we allow ourselves the time to examine its roots and learn about ourselves and our needs and dreams as well as our failures and shortcomings. This can, of course, become a pity party if we allow ourselves to stay stuck without using the appropriate tools given for recovery from depression.

All of these responses overlook the fact that depression is an illness. Unfortunately, when we believe the myths about depression, we gain downward momentum because we feel guilty for the darkness: because we can't snap out of it, because we must not be spiritual enough or we wouldn't be depressed, because we misunderstand the difference between depression and self-pity. Looking at underlying issues can bring clarity to the problem.

Underlying Issues

False guilt and self-blame can immobilize the depressive. Rooting out the hidden issues contributing to depression involves careful digging in the soil of our hearts. Some of these issues—stress, unforgiveness, grief—were developed more fully in my first book, *Quiet Places: A Woman's Guide to Personal Retreat* (Bethany House Publishers, 1997). Anger and worry are discussed later in this book.

Stress and trauma. Stress is a primary factor in psychologically induced depression, especially stress resulting from trauma or loss. Those suffering from chronic pain or serious or protracted illness are also susceptible to depression. Cancer treatment, as well as certain steroids, may lead to depression. Check with your physician if you are uncertain.

Past pain and grief. Depression is a warning, a message frozen in icy darkness: "Past pain buried here." Depression often veils us from our pain, from the grief necessary to recover from loss or change in our lives. In addition, people who had a loved one die when they were young are at least twice as likely to suffer from major depression as those who have not experienced a similar grief.[8] Grief is a natural and necessary means of moving out of a depression.

Fear. Fear can act as an effective catapult into depression. Fear of what others think of us, of authority figures, of failure, of imperfection, of physical danger: all these keep us self-contained and closed up, and can spring us right into the darkness.

Shame. Lewis Smedes writes, "I lugged around inside me a dead weight of not-good-enoughness."[9] This shame can plummet us like a weighted arrow into depression. Some characteristics of shame follow:

- Shame includes an enduring negative self-image.
- Shame is highly "performance conscious."
- Shame makes you unaware of personal boundaries.
- Shame festers in people who are "wounded."
- Shame is accompanied by a pervading tiredness.
- Shame has a built-in radar system, tuned to keeping everyone happy and at peace.
- Shame makes you ignore your own needs like a martyr.
- Shame tends toward addictive behavior, which can manifest itself in overinvolvement in work or ministry.
- Shame has no concept of "normal."
- Shame makes it difficult to trust others.
- Shame makes you possessive in relationships.
- Shame has a high need for control.[10]

Unforgiveness. Hauling unforgiveness around is like swimming with iron skillets for flippers. We know we're supposed to forgive, but sometimes our pride, or our pain over being hurt, prevents us from releasing both ourselves and the unforgiven of the burden. And so our souls sink under the weight, and the waters of depression cover our heads.

Loss of self. The more distanced we become from the person God created us to be, the more likely we are to become depressed. Years ago, when finally naming the pervasive darkness that surrounded me, I realized I had never understood the nameless yearning of my soul. Disguising—and avoiding—myself by excessively meeting others' needs, I lost myself, slipping into depression without recognizing the cave's damp shadows.

Anger. Pulling us into the vortex of depression may be anger: anger at ourselves, at others, at God. But because we're taught that anger isn't spiritual, or that nice girls don't get angry, we bury it, and as it tunnels into our soul, depression results. (Anger is covered more fully in a later chapter.)

Notice the strong interconnection between fear, rage, depression, and lack of control. Tracy Thompson writes,

> By this time, depression had taken over my brain, and sleep was its first casualty. I was an insomniac, irritable, raging at the slightest noise in the night, a caldron of anger during the day. After years of suppressing rage, I now felt like a volcano in continuous eruption. Any minor inconvenience could set me off—misplacing a blouse, getting lost somewhere . . . finding myself stalled in a traffic jam. I felt I was going out of control. My fear of doing so was at war with my overwhelming need to express this constant, nameless fury in some physical way. I threw things; I beat helplessly on the floor.[11]

Shaking free from some of the underlying causes of depression is no easy task.

Coping With Depression

Learning about ourselves is a principle tool for recovery from depression. At what times do we become depressed? Depression strikes when faith gets overwhelmed. Heavy responsibilities, busyness, and lack of sleep draw her to the darkness. For myself, this recent onset of depression followed three weeks of family illness and the resultant stress, bracketed by out-of-town company on both ends. The shadows crept closer with problems at work and fatigue, and when each child came home with school-related difficulties, I slipped into the darkness like a pebble in a mudslide.

Proper nutrition becomes a vital tool in balancing our systems, as do exercise and rest. Creating a safety net of strategic friends, joining a support group, seeking counseling, and consulting a physician to eliminate possible biological or neurological causes: all these will aid us in our efforts toward recovery. For Janice, therapy and half a tablet of an antidepressant gave her back her life. For Therese, an exercise routine and avoiding caffeine help her move toward the light.

One of the biggest problems with depression is that good self-care requires energy, a primary missing ingredient in the depressive. I scarcely have the stamina to go up and down the stairs, much less care for myself. Sleeping eight hours provides a base of rest out of which to begin positive self-care.

Besides learning about our own depression-starters, we must also begin to ask, "What makes me happy?" God does not desire for us to live with a flat-line of the soul. If denying my gifts emaciates my joy, then embracing them and seeking ways to employ them gives altitude to the horizontal EKG. If our hearts lighten around humor, then we need to place ourselves with funny people. If beauty restores our soul, then we must seek out the beauty around us.

The vicious downward spiral can be slowed and stopped by taking small steps in the darkness toward the light. Because, though our beds swim with tears in the dark, dawn always comes. God has set a faithful witness in the sky, testifying to the steadiness of His care for us. God promises joy in the morning.

Healing Light

My throat aches from swallowing my tears. My jaws clench tightly to keep the pain inside. I force myself to reach out to Rich, to hold and be held, to bridge the gap between dark and light, to share the dark so I no longer alienate him. With my head against his neck, a tear escapes, leaving a stream of silent despair down my face. His strong, silent support wraps around me, holding me in my darkness, an unwavering candle of faith and strength.

I have loved the darkness, embraced it, wallowed in it like a harlot; loved the darkness more than the light. But the darkness, which recedes and then sweeps back in to cover my head, I now push away, awaiting the brightness of the Christ, who said,

"I am the Light of the World."

Once, hiking in the Ozarks, a file of girls trickled past us, exclaiming over plate-sized leaves and tiny acorns and spring forest growth. At the end of the file, an older woman held the elbow of a slender reed of a girl. The girl walked carefully, listening as her guide helped her not only to walk but to see.

Darkness has blinded me, but I am beginning to cry with the blind men by the roadside, "Lord, we want you to restore our sight."

I determine to test recovery theories for depression. I will share my shadow-dappled soul with others, talk about the darkness with them. I will work through this. I will practice exerting my will, choosing to limit my distorted thinking, to eat well and to show up for exercise class, to pray and praise.

And so I sing. Warbly sounds work their way out around sobs. The song that comes to mind is from church on Sunday:

My hope is built on nothing less
than Jesus' blood and righteousness.
I dare not trust the sweetest frame
but wholly lean on Jesus' name. . . .
When darkness veils His lovely face,
I rest on His unchanging grace;
In ev'ry high and stormy gale
My anchor holds within the veil. . . .
His oath, His covenant, His blood
Support me in the whelming flood;
When all around my soul gives way,
He then is all my hope and stay.[12]

I imagine Jesus, holding me up, searching for me, calling my name, smiling all the while, and I weep. I, in this black hole of darkness, am being wooed by the Light. Not judged, not evaluated, but lovingly called out.

Just as God created the night, God created the potential for these dark, shadowy times of the soul. But God also created the light, that the night might be limited. We can barely pray in the sweeping darkness, "Lord, take the dimness of my soul away."[13] But it is enough.

"The Light shines in the darkness, but the darkness does not overcome it."

Quotes for Contemplation

Moods may persist long after the circumstances that triggered them have passed. When a mood outlives its context, it can become a serious liability to healthy emotional functioning. Individuals whose moods impair their work, relationships, and potential for happiness are said to have a mood disorder.

—MARY ELLEN COPELAND, M.S.,
THE DEPRESSION WORKBOOK

Here is a mental treatment guaranteed to cure every ill that man is heir to: Sit for half an hour every night and forgive anyone against whom you have any ill will.

—**CHARLES FILLMORE**

When depression is stigmatized as illness and weakness, a double bind is created: If we admit to depression, we will be stigmatized by others; if we feel it but do not admit it, we stigmatize ourselves, internalizing the social judgment. . . . The only remaining choice may be truly sick behavior: to experience no emotion at all.

—**LESLEY HAZELTON,**
THE RIGHT TO FEEL BAD

Letting the pain out was an upsetting but necessary part of getting free from the depression.

—**JAN DRAVECKY,**
A JOY I'D NEVER KNOWN

Perfectionists have the highest rate of depression among all human beings.

—**JOHN POWELL,**
HAPPINESS IS AN INSIDE JOB

Mental illness taught me that I can get really *ill relying on myself. Acknowledging God as a power higher than myself was all-important in my recovery. There's no doubt that God had a hand in the medication and the psychotherapy that helped me recover. But beyond such treatment, I have come to realize that prayer is where all healing begins—healing of the mind, the body, the spirit or the heart.*

—**A PSYCHIATRIST**

The way you live your life, take care of yourself, and feel about yourself affects mood instability and depression. They may be the whole problem, or may simply make matters worse. All the effort you direct toward alleviating stress in your life, making positive changes in your lifestyle, and changing your negative thought patterns to positive ones will enhance your overall well-being and help stabilize your moods.

—**MARY ELLEN COPELAND, M.S.,**
THE DEPRESSION WORKBOOK

I tore down the dark and dismal drapes

that hung like dead men on the gallows.
I threw open the windows
and cried out as the sunlight spilled into this
silent room
as surprised as I.
And as my eyes became accustomed
to this fierce and searching light,
I realized it was time to laugh again.

—**SHEILA WALSH,**
HONESTLY

Scriptures for Meditation

He sent from on high, He took me;
He drew me out of many waters.
He delivered me from my strong enemy,
and from those who hated me,
for they were too mighty for me.
They confronted me in the day of my calamity,
But the Lord was my stay.
He brought me forth also into a broad place;
He rescued me, because He delighted in me. . . .
For Thou dost light my lamp;
The Lord my God illumines my darkness.

—**PSALM 18:16–19, 21**

In the beginning was the Word, and the Word was with God, and the Word was God. He was in the beginning with God; all things were made through him, and without him was not anything made that was made. In him was life, and the life was the light of men. The light shines in the darkness, and the darkness has not overcome it.

—**JOHN 1:1–5 RSV**

The people who sat in darkness
have seen a great light,
and for those who sat
in the region and shadow of death
light has dawned.

—**MATTHEW 4:16 RSV**

But as for me,
I will watch expectantly for the Lord;
I will wait for the God of my salvation.
My God will hear me.
Do not rejoice over me, O my enemy.
Though I fall I will rise;
Though I dwell in darkness,
the Lord is a light for me.

—MICAH 7:7–8

For God, who said, "Light shall shine out of darkness," is the One who has shone in our hearts to give the light of the knowledge of the glory of God in the face of Christ.

But we have this treasure in earthen vessels, that the surpassing greatness of the power may be of God and not from ourselves; we are afflicted in every way, but not crushed; perplexed, but not despairing; persecuted, but not forsaken; struck down, but not destroyed; always carrying about in the body the dying of Jesus, that the life of Jesus also may be manifested in our body.

—2 CORINTHIANS 4:6–10

Journaling

Recording our journey while in the light helps us find our way in the dark. Take time now, illuminated by God's Word, to examine your experiences or the experiences of loved ones with depression. If you are currently in the valleys of depression, journaling can help you sort reality from distorted thinking. Remembering God's faithfulness in the past also throws light on the path.

Prayers of Confession, Praise, Petition

One of the most natural reactions to depression is to shut God out of our darkness, forgetting that "darkness and light are alike" to our Lord. Psalm 139:12 reads, "Even the darkness is not dark to Thee, and the night is as bright as the day. Darkness and light are alike to Thee."

God longs for you to pour out all that is in your heart. May you find healing as you enter God's presence.

Moments for Creation

Reflect on the interplay of dark and light, of sun and shadows, as you spend time in God's creation. Shady woods have green plants: there is growth in darkness. Places of dark are always fringed and highlighted by light. Let the Lord's handiwork illuminate your soul.

Silence

The psalmist states, "My soul waits in silence for God only; From Him is my salvation" (62:1). For the prophet Elijah, Yahweh came to him not in fire or fierce wind, but in the gentle sound of stillness. May God enfold you in the silence.

Questions for Reflection

1. What experiences have you had with depression? What preconceived notions have you had about depression? Does your family have a history of depression? How has depression impacted you physically, psychologically, emotionally, spiritually? How has it affected your family? Your friendships? What are some beginning signs that you are slipping into depression?

2. Depression and self-esteem dance in circles: Misunderstanding our value in God's eyes can lead us into depression; guilt for being depressed, thinking we must be defective, erodes our self-esteem. How has depression affected your feelings about your image in God's sight?

3. How do you feel about sharing times of depression with others in your life? Who can bring light into your darkness by their support and encouragement? How do you want your friends to help you when you are depressed?

4. What memories or incidents from the past seem related to the roots of depression that you are uncovering? Anger, fear, damaged self-esteem, shame? If there is depression in your family tree, how were you affected by that?

5. What steps is the Spirit nudging you to take regarding depression, whether yours or that of a loved one?

Hymn of Praise

Spirit of God, Descend Upon My Heart

Spirit of God, descend upon my heart;
wean it from earth; through all its pulses move;
stoop to my weakness, mighty as thou art,
and make me love thee as I ought to love.

I ask no dream, no prophet ecstasies,
no sudden rending of the veil of clay,
no angel visitant, no opening skies;
but take the dimness of my soul away.

Hast thou not bid me love thee, God and King?
All, all thine own, soul, heart and strength and mind.
I see thy cross; there teach my heart to cling.
O let me seek thee, and O let me find!

Teach me to feel that thou art always nigh;
teach me the struggles of the soul to bear.
To check the rising doubt, the rebel sigh,
teach me the patience of unanswered prayer.

Teach me to love thee as thine angels love,
one holy passion filling all my frame;
the kindling of the heaven-descended Dove,
my heart an altar, and thy love the flame.

—WORDS:
GEORGE CROLY, 1867

CHAPTER FIVE

Order Out of Chaos: Embracing Our God-Given Creativity

In a fast-paced world, we don't have much time for creativity. But God certainly took time, and why? Because of a great love for us! Here we explore the benefits of creativity and examine how we can incorporate creativity naturally into our lives without huge expenditures of effort or resources.

"What are you doing?" Rich's muffled voice came from behind the video camera. The children and I were knee-deep, literally, in cleaning the family room. Toys, games, action figures, and dress-up clothes filled the tiny viewing lens. My husband grinned as he waited for the obvious reply.

"Performing a creative act! We're bringing order out of chaos!" I declared triumphantly.

That creativity could transform the mundane was a miraculous discovery. In *Picked Up Pieces*, John Updike wrote, "Any activity becomes creative when the doer cares about doing it right, or better."[1] For years I languished under the impression that creativity was the conspicuous, flamboyant stuff: painting, composing, sculpting. I didn't write lyrics like Darlene, decorate like Karen, paint like Ellen, do calligraphy like Patti; therefore, my reasoning went, I must not be creative. Since I didn't dream up brilliant ads or marketing campaigns, I figured I was standing behind the door when God doled out creative gifts.

That creativity goes beyond the high-profile artistic forms, or even the dexterous use of a glue gun, was good news for me. My forms of creative expression were previously confined to stitching up clothes from ready-made patterns, which didn't fit my own limited and limiting definition of creativity.

Webster defines creativity as "to bring into existence; to invest with a new form, office, or rank." Maxine Hancock suggests that creativity is "finding new ways of putting existing components together to make a whole."[2]

There was a time when Christians were the forerunners in every area of media and market—when high ideals gave impetus to the highest, most creative quality of product. Today's attempts at "Christian" art and film-making are often embarrassingly inadequate. Creativity may be considered frivolous in the serious pursuit of life, liberty, and happiness, and irrelevant to one's spirituality. In the daily grind of earning a living and keeping a house, we shove creativity to the margins of our lives. And for the woman intent on serving God through church and community, the somber business of living a godly life can keep her so overcommitted she never fully embraces her God-given creativity. We have lost our edge in the world by relegating creativity to the arena of unnecessary and irrelevant.

Yet as I talk with women and listen to hidden dreams, frequently the desires buried in their hearts are dreams of expressing themselves more creatively, whether through the fine arts or their use of gifts and talents, time and treasures.

Too often we either don't think we're creative, don't understand the wide varieties of creative expression, or don't have good reasons to express our creativity.

So Who IS Creative?

Just because we don't paint like Monet doesn't mean we aren't creative individuals. God made something out of nothing, the ultimate form of creativity, bringing into existence the entire universe. A primary reason among women for not expressing creativity tends to be low self-esteem,[3] but examining our roots rules out that excuse. Because we are made in God's image, and God is creative, creativity is inherent in our very being, a basic component of our spiritual makeup.

Psychological testing seems to confirm this. Alex Osborn writes, "An analysis of almost all the psychological tests ever made points to the conclusion that creative talent is normally distributed—that *all* of us possess this talent."[4]

This is good news. Creativity is not a matter of feeling creative; it is a matter of fact. How could we, as children of the Creator God, *not* be creative? Creativity flows in us like sap in a tree. The question is not, then, "Are we creative?" but "How do we tap into this God-given trait?"

Types of Creativity

Thankfully, creativity goes beyond arts and crafts and fun with sequins. Much of our creativity we take for granted: putting a thousand meals on the table each year; juggling home, hearth, and workplace; living on a budget; and creating a loving, safe environment at home or work—all these require creativity whether we recognize it or not.

Creativity takes many forms. It is evident in words, actions, baking, hospitality, atmosphere, relationships. Many times I've trudged to the kitchen with twenty-five minutes to prepare a meal before the next scheduled event, only to recite the Rubietta version of the Mother Goose rhyme:

I went to the cupboard, the cupboard was bare!
What to prepare—there's no food anywhere!

After precious minutes of rummaging, like Merlin the magician I emerge from the kitchen with some unlikely combination and place a panic meal on the table. I'm rarely able to duplicate dishes because of this approach to meal planning, nor will my next publishing endeavor likely be a cookbook, but this seat-of-the-pants cooking creativity satisfies my last-minute tendencies and my basic dislike of advance planning.

Words are another arena of creative opportunity. You don't have to be a professional writer to use words well. In formless darkness, God spoke the world into existence! So, too, our words have the potential to create life, love, and laughter in the void of people's lives. Mother Teresa said,

"We are all pencils in the hand of God."

Marge sees her ministry as writing notes to people to affirm and encourage them. Only God knows the difference those letters have made in others' lonely lives. Sue's ability to turn negative commands into positive instruction opened my eyes to a new way to parent: Instead of barking, "Don't stand up on the slide!" she'd call out, "Let's stay on our seats when sliding, please!" Her example reminds me to check my ratio of negative and positive comments and creates a desire to build others up by emphasizing their good qualities. Relationships wither under sharpness but blossom with tender words. This blossoming is the heart of creativity.

As a rule, though, "how-to's" make me sleepy. My mind skitters off like a billiard ball on the rebound when discussions turn to crafts. But another's creative responses to life intrigue me. I can be passionate about turning pain into gain, finding a way out of a constricting situation, or turning a problem into praise.

Most fascinating is this creative response to life, to pain, and to adversity. In *The Courage to Create*, Rollo May writes that creativity "arises out of the struggle of human beings with and against that which limits them."[5] If, as Karen Mains says, creativity is "the ability to get away from the main track, break out of the mold, or diverge from the rest of society,"[6] then it would seem that creativity is a primary trait of the walk by faith, of a people who refused to let the world squeeze them into its mold (Rom. 12:2) and who wandered "in deserts and mountains and caves and holes in the ground" (Heb. 11:38).

Creativity and limits are defining, synergistic ingredients for us as Christians.

Creativity and Limits

Art museums, concert halls, and the patent office pulse with the work and names of people who refused to be constrained by their limitations but used them to create life. By age forty-six, Beethoven was completely deaf but went on to write some of his greatest compositions, including five symphonies. In spite of near blindness from cataracts, Monet painted until on death's doorstep. A blind Milton penned *Paradise Lost*. Rescued from her dark, silent world by a loving teacher, Helen Keller spent a lifetime giving hope to the blind and deaf. These people refused to be limited by life's limitations.

Research supports the notion that creativity is sharpened on the whetstone of adversity. So much of creativity is choosing to look for—and celebrate—life in the midst of what feels like death. Creativity is pressed into service when our backs are against the wall. When we are most limited, God is most free.

Pam's original Christmas celebration ideas arose out of her own limited time and energy: In a season of emotional and physical exhaustion, she declared that the tree would be for the birds. (It would only have things for the birds on it.) This saved her the holiday hassle and headache of decorating. She and her girls decorated with little bags of birdseed, suet, and anything else related to the feathery things fluttering in their wooded yard. At the end of the Christmas season, the entire tree went outside for the birds.

Years ago Rich phoned home after a meeting with what seemed like the worst possible news at the time. With profound discouragement he shared that a proposal toward which he had worked for several years had been rejected and that the alternate plan would require intense effort on his part and at least another two years' turnaround time.

Sensing God at work, I determined to create a festive meal. Later as the family gathered at the table, I lit the candles and, in a voice choked with tears, declared, "This is a celebration dinner. Even though we can't exactly celebrate Daddy's news, we CAN celebrate what we know: that God is in charge, that He has a better plan, and that we'll be better people because of the change."

The defining element that turns a limitation into creativity is attitude. This is summed up beautifully in Paul's words, "Whatever you do, do your work heartily, as for the Lord rather than for men; knowing that from the Lord you will receive the reward of the inheritance. It is the Lord Christ whom you serve" (Col. 3:23–24). And attitude is always adjustable, amazingly, by exercising our creativity.

Benefits of Creativity

Researchers have found that a creative "workout" lowers stress, builds self-confidence, and increases the enjoyment of life. Exercising our creativity may also affect our immune function, improve our health, and increase our longevity.[7] Remember the pride of bringing home a special project from school as a child? Fast-forward to the adult years: One reason that many women's groups, retirement centers, and nursing homes include a craft time in their meetings or schedules is because of these immediate benefits. When Gerald, who has Alzheimer's disease, disappears, his wife now knows to look for him in his workshop. Even though the electrical gadgets he tinkers with no longer work, simply participating in a creative act brings Gerald a lightness of heart and a sense of value.

Perhaps the greatest benefit of developing our creativity is that it brings us closer to the creative heart of God. Finding new ways to nurture that creativity is appealing.

Nurturing Creativity

Be curious. Albert Einstein said, "The important thing is not to stop questioning." Children are experts at this; as we age our curiosity becomes stunted or silenced by busyness and responsibility, or by shaming statements from others. To boost our creativity, ask "Why?" or "How do you know that?"; challenge assumptions; or take an opposing viewpoint on an issue.

Reflect. Journaling has jump-started my creativity because I'm forced to put my life, impressions, and feelings into words. As I reflect on life, I find that I listen to and look at the world around me with new eyes and ears. Creativity comes alive in the quiet.

Exercise. Aerobic exercise increases creativity, possibly due to changes in brain chemistry. In addition to releasing mood-elevating endorphins, the steady left-right pumping of our legs in exercise limbers up the creative right side of the brain, allowing the mind to free-associate. New ideas and combinations and solutions stream along with the increased blood flow. In her book *The Artist's Way*, Julia Cameron suggests that twenty minutes a day is long enough to get the creative juices flowing.[8]

Be spontaneous. Creativity is also freed by spontaneity, by not being afraid to play, to shift gears in midstream, or to change plans. For the controlling person, this is a hard task. When a handsome college graduate invited me to a banquet, my first thought was, "Absolutely not!" Then spontaneity came to my rescue, and thus began the most creative adventure of my life. (I married him. Good thing I said yes to the banquet.)

Laugh. Is there any more creative response to life than laughter? When Carol faced a difficult day, she prayed, "Lord, let me laugh through my day." And she did. Easily. Calvin Miller, a prolific author, says that much of his writing was conceived while laughing and playing. Looking for humor in a tight situation will change our outlook and may even bring up a solution.

Feel your feelings. Alexander Pope said in 1717, "He best can paint them who shall feel them most." Clueing into the internal world enhances our creativity, clears our minds, and opens us up to possibility.

Living Creatively

When we tap into the creativity that's as natural as oxygen in the blood, the creativity we're born with, the creativity of the Creator, our very lives will declare the glory of God. By embracing our God-given creativity, our lives can shine as beacons in a dark world, giving hope to those lost in darkness. When the lives and work of people who claim Christ as their Savior demonstrate the creativity of their Creator, people will notice. And a watching and waiting world will be led to the most creative and thorough redemption of all time.

Quotes for Contemplation

Flair is a creative expression God has imprinted on our souls. Yet we Christians are wary of those dramatic touches of finesse. God is not afraid to display his creativity; if we decorated a room in our home copying the glorious colors of just one of his sunsets, people would think we were outrageous. Yet he has donned his world with style and class, exquisite taste, breathtaking color combinations, scintillating humor. (Have you ever looked at the rear end of a baboon?) And he allows this repetition of glory and delightful surprise in his human creatures, as long as we don't slip into the error of thinking it is all of ourselves.

—KAREN MAINS,
OPEN HEART, OPEN HOME

A man or a woman without hope in the future cannot live creatively in the present.

—HENRI NOUWEN,
OUT OF SOLITUDE

I have no special gift. I am only passionately curious.

—ALBERT EINSTEIN

Every child is an artist. The problem is how to remain an artist once he grows up.

—**PABLO PICASSO**

The essence of invention isn't process but purpose. . . . Invention often occurs not because a person tries to be original, but because the person attempts to do something difficult.

—**D. N. PERKINS,**
PSYCHOLOGIST

No amount of skillful invention can replace the essential element of imagination.

—**EDWARD HOPPER**

Imagination is more important than knowledge.

—**ALBERT EINSTEIN**

Scriptures for Meditation

In the beginning God created the heavens and the earth. And the earth was formless and void, and darkness was over the surface of the deep; and the Spirit of God was moving over the surface of the waters. Then God said, "Let there be light"; and there was light. And God saw that the light was good.

—**GENESIS 1:1–4**

Then God said, "Let Us make man in Our image, according to Our likeness. . . . And God created man in His own image, in the image of God He created him; male and female He created them. And God blessed them; and God said to them, "Be fruitful. . . ."

—**GENESIS 1:26, 27–28**

Let the favor of the Lord our God be upon us;
And do confirm for us the work of our hands;
Yes, confirm the work of our hands.

—**PSALM 90:17**

The heavens declare the glory of God;

the skies proclaim the work of his hands.

—PSALM 19:1 NIV

I urge you therefore . . . by the mercies of God, to present your bodies a living and holy sacrifice, acceptable to God, which is your spiritual service of worship. And do not be conformed to this world, but be transformed by the renewing of your mind, that you may prove what the will of God is, that which is good and acceptable and perfect.

—ROMANS 12:1–2

Journaling

The rote act of journaling with its repetitive movement of the hand frees up the right brain. Today as you journal, consider how you see creativity operating in your life. Write quickly, without censoring whatever comes to mind about creativity: yours, God's, another's.

Prayers of Confession, Praise, Petition

Sin can hinder our creativity. As you pause, invite the Holy Spirit to bring to mind any hidden sins, and confess them. Take time to move into a time of praise, thanksgiving, and adoration before laying all of your petitions at the foot of the cross.

Moments for Creation

Today as you move about in God's created glory, let the incredible creativity of the Creator inspire you with awe. What strikes you in particular as you observe God's handiwork? How does it teach you about God?

Silence

Let the times of observation and praise move you into silent adoration of God. As you lift your heart toward Him, may He envelop you with His presence.

Questions for Reflection

1. Creativity is a fragile endowment at birth, and easily snuffed out in childhood. It is often considered impractical. What messages did you

receive/perceive as a child about creativity? How was it nurtured in you?

2. Where do you see creativity operating in your life right now? What are you good at doing? What activities or tasks make you feel renewed? What would you consider one of your greatest stumbling blocks to creativity?

3. What friendships energize you, sparking your creativity, lifting you to a higher plain? Which ones deflate and de-energize you? How can you make the most of the relationships you have and seek out new friendships that uplift, fulfill, and challenge you?

4. How do you really feel about creativity: is it fluff, inconsequential, to be relegated to the realm of excess and luxury? How do your feelings fit with what you see God displaying from border to border of the visible world?

5. What areas in your life call for a creative response?

Hymn of Praise

GOD, WHO STRETCHED THE SPANGLED HEAVENS

(to the tune of "Joyful, Joyful, We Adore Thee")

God, who stretched the spangled heavens,

infinite in time and place,
flung the suns in burning radiance
through the silent fields of space,
we your children,
in your likeness,
share inventive powers with you.
Great Creator, still creating,
show us what we yet may do.

Proudly rise our modern cities,
stately buildings, row on row;
yet their windows, blank, unfeeling,
stare on canyoned streets below,
where the lonely oft drift unnoticed
in the city's ebb and flow,
lost to purpose and to meaning,
scarcely caring where they go.

We have ventured worlds undreamed of
since the childhood of our race;
known the ecstasy of winging
through untraveled realms of space;
probed the secrets of the atom,
yielding unimagined power,
facing us with life's destruction
or our most triumphant hour.

As each far horizon beckons,
may it challenge us anew,
children of creative purpose,
serving others, honoring you.
May our dreams prove rich with promise,
each endeavor well begun.
Great Creator, give us guidance
till our goals and yours are one.

—WORDS: CATHERINE CAMERON, 1967

CHAPTER SIX

Taming the Lion: Anger Within Limits

Anger can be a surprisingly helpful emotion, clueing us in to our need to be loved, valued, appreciated—or in charge. Learn how to recognize the benefits of anger and what to do about it.

Karen clutched her anger to her breast. Stuffing each indignation into the suitcase of her soul like a warrior gathering ammunition for battle, she felt the power of the righteous against the sinner. She was right to be angry over a co-worker's imperfections. Karen stashed the anger suitcase in her closet, filling it for a full year. Lateness. Forgetfulness. Unreasonable requests. How dare she talk to Karen about improving *her* work?! On and on went the grievances, drops of water that became a roaring, raging waterfall when she pulled out the suitcase and spilled its contents over the supervisor's lap. Karen reveled in anger's power, had the satisfaction of seeing the accumulation of that anger poison their supervisor's feelings against her co-worker.

Yes, anger empowered Karen. To wound another, all the while feeling better, justified, righteous, about herself. In the end, her supervisor asked about each complaint, "What did you do about this at the time?"

Karen looked down at the table, surprised. "Nothing."

"Did you talk to your colleague about her lateness here?"

"Yes," she mumbled.

"Then why are you bringing it before me now? Is this a chronic problem, or do you see improvement?"

Drop by drop, the supervisor evaluated the evidence of the co-worker's imperfections and found her human.

Karen used anger to hurt another rather than to heal. Anger festered in that suitcase, daily growing more rank and radioactive. Fortunately for her associate, the supervisor saw the problems for what they were. Unfortunately for Karen, she contaminated herself, her soul, and a working relationship that could have helped her mature both professionally and personally. Anger could have helped her develop relationship skills and better herself through examining her own reaction to minor problems. Instead, it stunted her maturity. Anger could have helped another grow through honest, gentle confrontation. Instead, locked up, it assumed potentially lethal power. Karen poisoned the department, talking about her grievances with everyone—except the co-worker. Anger fanned the fires of discontent rather than fueling a positive atmosphere.

Women are raised to suppress or deny anger. We grow up believing that "ladies do not get angry." We "make nice." Sheila Walsh writes in *Honestly*, "If a man is angry, he is often viewed as a man of passion, of principle, but an angry woman is quite another matter. It is too easy to dismiss her as neurotic or strident."[1] Some Christians go so far as to say that we should never be angry, because we can never approximate the righteousness that Jesus revealed in His anger in the Temple. And we certainly should never be angry at God. We learn early in life that anger is the enemy, to be avoided at all costs.

Unfortunately, as Karen learned, those costs can be high.

The High Price of Harboring Anger

Anger often travels incognito, disguised in a more acceptable costume. Perhaps Karen didn't recognize anger or its costs. Sarcasm masks anger, as does rudeness. Some of anger's closest kin include resentment, prejudice, and sadness. Digging around in the soil of my own self-pity and jealousy, I was surprised to uncover anger at their roots.

As a connoisseur of the fine art of being angry and staying angry, I've found some residual effects of anger. Sleep loss, for instance. It's hard to sleep with the mouth drawn into a thin, livid line and the heart thudding madly. In fact, loss of sleep can be symptomatic of anger, easily leading into depression—another sign of misplaced or misused anger. Further, studies reveal that . . .

> . . . people who respond to anger in a hostile manner and see others' motives as antagonistic have an increased risk of coronary disease and suffer a higher mortality rate in general.[2]

The original word in Latin for anger meant *to strangle*, and anger, used improperly, throttles its victims. Anger separates us from ourselves, God, and others. When anger stays on the inside, we're robbed of energy needed to set goals, live deliberately, and be present to loved ones and to God.

Even with the costs of anger on our health, our soul, and our relationships, it too often reigns.

Recognizing Anger and Its Roots

Anger covers a wide spectrum of behavior: stuffing it, denying it, or spewing its venom on the nearest target. From rage and violence to rigid frozenness, anger is rarely expressed in helpful ways. Unacknowledged or unexpressed, nurtured by a stream of strident self-talk, anger spreads in the fertile burial ground of the soul—its roots fast-growing and tenacious, squeezing the life out of its victims in the forms of resentment and unforgiveness. Why don't we let anger teach us and others? At the root of anger is often fear: fear of alienating others or destroying relationships; fear of rejection, abandonment, or other consequences of being honest about our feelings; fear that we will lose control of the anger and hurt someone; or fear that we will misuse it as we've experienced its misuse.

Psychologists call this fear *endangerment*. Daniel Goldman writes,

> A universal trigger for anger is the sense of being endangered. Endangerment can be signaled not just by an outright physical threat but also, as is more often the case, by a symbolic threat to self-esteem or dignity: being treated unjustly or rudely, being insulted or demeaned, being frustrated in pursuing an important goal.[3]

Because the side effects are so severe, we must be receiving some rewards from retaining our anger.

Negative Benefits of Anger

With so many problems associated with irresponsible ire, why do we avoid a face-off with anger? As a mother, I've noticed my children often react angrily when they feel threatened, powerless, or unloved. The same is true of adults. Anger is also an attempt to gain or reestablish control and power, to deflect focus from our own failings, or to feel better about ourselves (at another's expense). It can also be a response to being hurt by another.

Thus, anger keeps us safe, especially if we fear change or personal growth. It helps us beat back other painful emotions we're afraid will burn us, like firefighters beating back a brush fire in a drought. Anger keeps pain at bay, masking the real issues. Anger may bring about another's obedience, as in our children, though it may also bring their fear and hatred. Anger provides energy by tapping into the adrenaline stored for our "fight or flight" reactions. It also keeps us in the center of our world, others spinning out around our egos centrifugally. This may explain why some consider anger a selfish emotion. It may be God-given, but in our hands it easily becomes impulse-driven.

When we nurse anger, it morphs into a parasite, a tick swollen and bloated, feeding on our lifeblood, sucking out our energy and contentment and joy. Misused, ignored, or stored, anger easily slips into sin.

Be Angry but Do Not Sin

When anger

- separates me from God, or
- begins to control me, or
- occupies my every thought, or
- becomes a weapon for harming another, attacking people rather than problems,

it has fermented into sin.

Solomon was right in saying, "Anger resides in the bosom of fools," (Eccl. 7:9) for when anger lodges in our souls, God is evicted. Far better to adhere to Paul's advice, "Be angry, and yet do not sin. Do not let the sun go down on your anger" (Eph. 4:26). Dealing with anger appropriately, when reactions and passions have cooled, does not give the Evil One the chance to turn a natural emotion into sin.

Identified and defused, anger can lead us to maturity, propelling us toward making needed changes in our lives, our routines, our habits. Anger becomes our friend.

Anger the Ally

Anger is a white-gloved servant, handing us an engraved invitation to grow. Anger becomes a useful implement in the Master's toolbox when it helps us realize that something is wrong, something isn't working. Anger points out unfinished business from the past; directs us to areas in our daily lives that need work; alerts us to our needs, desires, and dreams; and helps us recognize where we need to establish boundaries.

Linea's story demonstrates this.

Flashbacks and Flashfires

The scene replayed endlessly in Linea's mind. How had the anger gotten so far out of control? She'd grown up with violence and had determined not to use any form of hitting when disciplining her children. But sometimes the anger boiled up within and she *reacted* rather than *responded* to disobedience or disrespect.

In this case, her older son's careless attitude and ugly demeanor got to her, and when he cruelly rejected some loving attention from his little brother, she went after him. Grabbed him. Wanted to strike until something in him changed. Instead, she tried to simply restrain him, to hold out against his violence. It escalated, and the struggle became real.

Later, asking herself "Why?," Linea suddenly saw herself as a young child, ignored, emotionally abused, rejected. No one stood up for her. And that neglected, orphaned child still lived within her. Seeing the same pattern repeated between her boys, she had become the avenging mother she'd never had, defending the younger from the older brother's words, from the wounds of rejections that would never fade.

To avoid repeating the scene, she and her son devised a contract. They both determined to allow a cooling off period when reactions flared. He agreed not to leave a discussion, and she agreed not to touch him in anger. Together they are slowly carving out a new relationship. And because Linea listened to the anger, she realized that the past pain was hurting her current relationships and began to seek healing.

Anger, which came out as a curse, began to be a blessing, leading to reconciliation and hope.

Anger and the Amygdala

Do words ever zip from your mouth to lash another; does your hand ever strike out, leaving an imprint on another's cheek? Occasionally, I react emotionally and hotly to another's words or actions, only to wonder later, "What was that all about?" And after prayer, silence, journaling, and general soul searching, I come up empty. I cannot uncover the roots of my wrath.

Recent brain research helps clarify some of these flash reactions. The difference between a reaction (acting or speaking without thinking) and a response (a measured, thoughtful action) may be found in the mind's neural pathways. The brain stores fact and feeling memories in different places. Feeling memories are warehoused in the amygdala, whereas facts and rational impressions are sent to the neocortex, or the thinking brain.

When an emotionally charged incident occurs, the two different routes register a response in our brains. Immediately, the information is telegraphed to the amygdala, which scans all available files of impressions for similarity and then blasts a reaction to our consciousness. The slower route delivers the message through the neocortex, deliberately sorting facts, gathering information like a reporter, then generating a rational response. The speedier messenger service is vital in life-or-death situations calling for immediate action. Unfortunately, it is too easy to rely on the "gut instinct" and ignore the thinking brain's measured response.

Interestingly, the higher a person's emotional intelligence, the less often she relies on the amygdala's news flashes, except in situations that warrant a flash reaction. Much of present-day counseling and psychotherapy are actually times of merging the helpful parts of the amygdala with the neocortex; retraining rampant emotions to move rationally through the thinking brain. Thankfully, anger, rage, and their shady kinfolk can be retrained, restrained, and redirected by defusing.

Anger Inventory

- Do you say that others make you angry?
- Do you justify your anger by blaming it on circumstances or pressures around you?
- Do you attack those closest to you?
- Are you afraid of accepting responsibility for your actions?
- Have you accepted anger as a way of life?[4]

Defusing Anger

1. Calm down through breathing, praying, waiting, and self-talk ("Help me, God! This is rough but I can handle this," etc.). Distraction, exercise, and hard work dissipate anger, provided we shift thinking gears to a less toxic subject. Research shows a minimum of twenty minutes is necessary for the flooding emotions and resultant heart rate increase to reach normal levels and reduce rage-related incidents.

2. Listen to what the other is really saying. This dilutes an angry response. Daniel Goldman writes,

> A handful of emotional competences—mainly being able to calm down (and calm your partner), empathy, and listening well—can make it more likely a couple will settle their disagreements effectively.[5]

In relationships, I'm trying to get beyond the *way* others express themselves, whether they are rude or disrespectful, so I can hear their real feelings. This short-circuits the emotional charge.

3. Look for the meaning and emotional memory behind your anger. Ask yourself: Why am I angry? Do I feel threatened or unsafe? Powerless or hurt? Insecure? A sense of low self-esteem or injustice? Does this resemble anything in the past?

4. Let the journal be an emotional halfway house. Writing our rage reduces its power and gives clarity and perspective.

5. Express anger selectively. Before you confront the person with whom you are angry, ask yourself, "Is this problem a pattern? Is it worth making an issue over?" Take time to gain perspective: Yelling at the cashier because you feel diminished by her rudeness may be less wise than addressing a family member who habitually treats you rudely.

6. Anger is not impotent. If we can't confront, we can still uproot bitterness and unforgiveness. God knows we're angry. Pray and sing the anger. Shout a psalm—David did, and was still declared a man after God's own heart.

Anger, Grief, and God

One root word for anger is the Old Norse *angr*, which means grief. Anger is a natural stage in grief recovery. Unlike most other stages of grief, anger provides energy, so staying angry is easier than working past the anger and through the grief, processing the underlying pain. Chronic anger may camouflage arrested grief.

Another natural tendency is to assume that if someone hurts us they must not like us. This becomes a spiritual issue, because the assumption logically follows that if bad things happen to us, God must not love us, either. Though this assumption flaunts all the gentle nurturing God has done for us, anger does bubble up and, unacknowledged, drives a wedge between us and God. In spite of childhood and church warnings about NOT harboring anger at God, the Scriptures record instances of people regaling God with their grievances against Him.

In the book of Jonah, Jonah's anger toward God, in chapter four, taught Jonah about himself and about God. Elijah, too, was tired and angry after waging spiritual warfare, and stood at the mouth of a cave airing his anger at God. God did not abandon Elijah, but instead brought a companion to minister to him. God responded in a nurturing manner to Elijah's anger. (1 Kings 19:14–21)

Anger and Godliness

Anger can be a surprisingly helpful emotion. When we recognize, understand, deal with, and release anger, we win. We walk away with a clean slate, purged of bitterness, having warded off any possibility of resentment's radioactive buildup.

Harbored, anger holds us prisoner.

Hurled, anger hurts others, impaling them with our poisonous arrows.

Handled constructively, anger brings growth and godliness.

Quotes for Contemplation

A part of the quiet rage I experienced was anger against God. Inwardly and very quietly, I raved and ranted against Him in my spirit. I think it's better to get angry at God than to walk away from Him. It's better to honestly confront our feelings and let Him know this is how we feel—this is awful, my pillow is wet from all my tears, I'm sick and tired of this, and I can't stand it one more minute.

—JONI EARECKSON TADA,
IN *DARK CLOUDS, SILVER LININGS*

Emotional maturity is the ability to know what it is that I am feeling, what its name is, then to discover positive channels for it. The quicker the process operates in us, the more mature we are becoming. Spiritual maturity requires that we submit to this procedure before the Lord.

—KAREN MAINS,
KAREN KAREN

I was angry with my friend:
I told my wrath, my wrath did end.
I was angry with my foe:
I told it not, my wrath did grow.

And I watered it in fears,
Night and morning with my tears;
And I sunned it with smiles,
And with soft deceitful wiles.

And it grew both day and night,
Till it bore an apple bright.
And my foe beheld it shine,
And he knew that it was mine.

And into my garden stole,
When the night had veiled the pole;
In the morning glad I see
My foe outstretched beneath the tree.

—WILLIAM BLAKE,
"A POISON TREE," 1794

In a 1990 study of 192 married couples, University of Michigan researchers found that in households where both partners suppressed angry feelings, the wives had a significantly higher mortality rate than women in relationships where anger was openly expressed. For their part, the men remained oblivious. Their longevity showed no relation to wives' anger. . . . [Another study found that] people who regularly quashed their anger were more than twice as likely to die in the next twelve years as people who recognized and expressed angry feelings.

—ALLISON GLOCK,
SPECIAL REPORT, WHITE
COMMUNICATIONS

If another's words about us determine our sense of self, then we might natrually feel angry about perceived criticism.

—**JANE RUBIETTA**

In using our anger as a guide to determining our innermost needs, values, and priorities, we should not be distressed if we discover just how unclear we are. If we feel chronically angry or bitter in an important relationship, this is a signal that too much of the self has been compromised and we are uncertain about what new position to take or what options we have available to us. To recognize our lack of clarity is not a weakness but an opportunity, a challenge, and a strength. . . . It is an act of courage to acknowledge our own uncertainty and sit with it for a while. . . . Our anger can be a powerful vehicle for personal growth and change if it does nothing more than help us recognize that we are not yet clear about something and that it is our job to keep struggling with it.

—**HARRIET GOLDHOR LERNER, PH.D., THE DANCE OF ANGER**

Anger . . . [is] a feeling that we often suppress because it is so uncomfortable for us. In our chaotic homes, the turmoil was so intense that we learned to deny our anger. We felt safer not expressing our anger and hoped it would go away. We eventually became unaware of its presence. Repressed anger leads to serious resentment and depression. It causes physical complications that lead to stress-related illnesses. Denying anger causes problems in relationships because we are not being truthful about our feelings. We are fearful of alienating people and destroying relationships.

—**RECOVERY PUBLICATIONS, THE TWELVE STEPS—A WAY OUT**

The key to becoming unstuck, to getting control of our anger, is changing our negative self-talk to positive self-talk. To change the way we feel, we must change the way we think. . . . Self-pity is caused by negative self-talk. Self-pity is anger, plain and simple. We're angry that life isn't fair, that it's full of hardship and disappointment. We think of ourselves as victims. . . . We cope with our problems by learning to be accountable for our own happiness.

—**GAYLE ROSELLINI AND MARK WORDEN, OF COURSE YOU'RE ANGRY**

Scriptures for Meditation

Everyone should be quick to listen, slow to speak and slow to become angry, for man's anger does not bring about the righteous life that God desires. . . . If anyone considers himself religious and yet does not keep a tight rein on his tongue, he deceives himself and his religion is worthless.

—JAMES 1:19–20, 26 NIV

Do not be quickly provoked in your spirit, for anger resides in the lap of fools.

—ECCLESIASTES 7:9 NIV

Go ahead and be angry. You do well to be angry—but don't use your anger as fuel for revenge. And don't stay angry. Don't go to bed angry. Don't give the Devil that kind of foothold in your life. . . .

Watch the way you talk. Let nothing foul or dirty come out of your mouth. Say only what helps, each word a gift.

Don't grieve God. Don't break his heart. His Holy Spirit, moving and breathing in you, is the most intimate part of your life, making you fit for himself. Don't take such a gift for granted.

Make a clean break with all cutting, backbiting, profane talk. Be gentle with one another, sensitive. Forgive one another as quickly and thoroughly as God in Christ forgave you.

—EPHESIANS 4:26–32
THE MESSAGE

An angry man stirs up dissension, and a hot-tempered one commits many sins.

—PROVERBS 29:22 NIV

He who restrains his words has knowledge and he who has a cool spirit is a man of understanding.

—PROVERBS 17:27 NIV

Journaling

What residual anger items lodge in the suitcase of your soul? Write them down, purging yourself of the contamination, then spread them out before God.

Prayers of Confession, Praise, Petition

Knowing that God sees our souls frees us to seek forgiveness through confession and generates praise from clean hearts. What joy, then, to lay our burdens and petitions before the Lord, trusting that He loves us and our loved ones more than we can imagine, and desires the very best for us.

Moments for Creation

Looking at the created world outside lets us know, without a doubt, that God is loving and righteous altogether. Invite God along on a stroll, and delight in His goodness as revealed in creation.

Silence

Look over Scriptures that have spoken to you today. What would our Savior speak into your heart as you humble yourself in silence before Him?

Questions for Reflection

1. How was anger handled in your childhood? Do you see yourself following parental patterns or going in the opposite direction?

2. How do you feel about expressing anger at God? What have you been taught about being angry with God? When have you been angry with Him?

3. When do you feel most angry? What does your anger camouflage? Can you identify a feeling that precedes your anger, such as fear, unsafe feelings, low self-esteem, injustice, or a misplaced need for control?

4. How do you act out your anger? Spend money? Eat (or don't eat) emotionally? Deprive yourself? Slam doors, cabinets? Yell? Redirect it or transfer it to others? Stuff it in till you implode, explode, get sick? Since anger appears to be a God-given emotion, how would you like to handle your anger?

5. Might you be halted in the anger stage of the grieving process? What losses might you be grieving? Where is God in the midst of that process?

Hymn of Praise

A MIGHTY FORTRESS IS OUR GOD

A mighty fortress is our God,
a bulwark never failing;
our helper he amid the flood
of mortal ills prevailing.
For still our ancient foe
doth seek to work us woe;
his craft and power are great,
and armed with cruel hate,
on earth is not his equal.

Did we in our own strength confide,
our striving would be losing,
were not the right man on our side,
the man of God's own choosing.
Dost ask who that may be?
Christ Jesus, it is he;
Lord Sabaoth, his name,
from age to age the same,
and he must win the battle.

And though this world with devils filled,
should threaten to undo us,
we will not fear for God hath willed
his truth to triumph through us.
The Prince of Darkness grim,
we tremble not for him;
his rage we can endure,
for lo, his doom is sure;
one little word shall fell him.

That word above all earthly powers,
no thanks to them abideth;
the Spirit and the gifts are ours,
thru him who with us sideth.
Let goods and kindred go,
this mortal life also;
the body they may kill;
God's truth abideth still;
his kingdom is forever.

—MARTIN LUTHER, 1529

CHAPTER SEVEN

Get a Grip: Control

"If you want to make God laugh," says a friend, "just tell Him your plans." We wouldn't presume to dictate how God should run the world, but we exhaust ourselves trying to control everyone and everything when in reality we can rarely even control ourselves. Discover how to give up imaginary reins of control and find peace.

Footsteps thudded and reverberated as we tromped up the metal stairway leading to a tourist attraction. As captain by popular vote (mine), I kept the children in line by a steady stream of commands. "Hold on to the handrail. Look over there! Don't shove." The fact that my tour group was all related to me lent my commands credibility. They had to obey. I was kin.

On the downward trip, little legs were tired. One of the children spied the sign for the elevator. "Look! Let's ride the rest of the way."

But I was adamant. This wasn't part of the plan. "Read the rest of the sign. *Use only in emergencies.*" One of my own little legalisms was never to ride elevators when you can use stairs. On we clumped, despite huffs, puffs, and eyes rolling in irritation. The lecture continued. "Nothing wrong with our legs. Besides, what if we were on the elevator, and someone really needed it and couldn't ride it?" *Thud, thud, thud.*

At the bottom of the stairs, a gaggle of little guys, unsupervised, poked at the elevator button. I assumed the best: they didn't know how to read. "Hey, guys, the sign says to use only in emergencies."

They looked at me, eyes wide with disbelief and something else. Scorn, perhaps. One jabbed the button again. My Policewoman of the World role came to my rescue. "Look, boys, let's be obedient. . . ."

My children shrank back in embarrassment. My cousin cleared her throat and flashed her dark, horrified eyes at me. Niece and nephew tried to disappear into the metal siding behind us. I tried another tactic: false concern. "Is this an emergency?"

The elevator doors shuddered open, and the wide-eyed boys leapt to safety. When the doors began to shut, I might have tried to follow them, demanding good citizenship, if my cousin hadn't yanked me away.

Control

It's all about control. The effort to regulate—to exercise restraining or directing influence over another. My efforts are global: I try to control my husband, my children, the mail carrier, my friend, my politician, the credit card company. Once, at a mall, I even approached an older woman who had parked in the handicapped spot. I wasn't sure she deserved to park there! I am appalled by the demeaning effect of my controlling and by the message it sends: that I know best and others are ignorant and brainless.

Characteristics of Controllers

Controlling people tend to be those who feel powerless in other areas of their lives or who felt powerless as children. For instance, a wife whose husband is out of control may squeeze the life out of her children. Demanding that the world fit into our preconceived—and thus correct—understanding and interpretation, controllers are afraid of changes in plans, of having fun. In *The Twelve Steps—A Way Out*, the description for control reads,

> As children, we had little control over our environment or the

> events that took place in our lives. As adults, we control our feelings and behavior, and we try to control the feelings and behavior of others. We become rigid, manipulative, and we lack spontaneity in our lives. There is an element of distrust in our need to control. We trust only ourselves to carry out a task or to handle a situation. We manipulate others in order to manage their impressions of us, and we keep a balance that feels safe for us. We fear that our lives will get worse if we let go of control. We become stressed and anxious when control is not possible.[1]

These dark characteristics of controllers are lived out in a variety of ways.

Symptoms of Control

Control, for Lynda, shows up in her housekeeping. Her home is immaculate, desk free of clutter. She is organized almost to the point of obsessiveness. "But if my home is a mess, I feel out of control," she protests. Helga dreads bedtime with her husband because losing control during sex frightens her. Deborah finds that control is the real issue behind her nurturing, when she's rushing to take care of another's problems.

Bonnie takes on more projects, saying yes when she should say no. She's afraid to delegate. Nor does she like other controllers. Once she admitted wryly, watching a co-worker deliver an incomplete and poorly compiled project for the task force Bonnie headed, "I was afraid of this. That's why I try to do everything, because I know how to do it right." Micromanagement on the job, at home, and in the church is also thinly veiled control. When we need to have every detail checked, supervised, and perfect, we are controlling.

For Christie, control looks like "appearance management": trying to regulate another's impression of her or her children by the way she dresses her family. When her daughter protests over the ruffled blouse or the bows in her hair, Christie reminds her, "What other people think of us is very important, and they often decide what they think based on our clothes." I have shamed my children in precisely the same way.

These behaviors seem so positive: helping others, keeping a neat living environment, being super responsible at work, watching over our children. At face value they are positive behaviors, but it's like decorating a steel girder. We dress up the underlying reasons for our control, convinced that the best of intentions motivates us. I must constantly ask myself, "Is my concern caretaking or control? Where is the bisecting line between the extremes of control and negligence?"

My parenting, for instance, becomes controlling when I want to make my children into my image of what is acceptable, when my actions stem from fear for my own reputation, when I don't trust them to handle a circumstance. When I always want situations to turn out in my favor—my cries for justice!—I usually am guilty of controlling.

We attempt control in other ways, too: with shame, sex, approval, money, anger, affection, physical punishment, silence, emotional withdrawal, condemnation, or judgment. Unfortunately, our controlling ways devastate relationships.

Side Effects of Controlling

If my way is the only right way, then controlling implies judgment and lack of trust. Such messages do incalculable damage to my relationships and to my soul. Questioning every penny another spends, I telegraph, "You are a failure with money, and I don't trust you. You make bad choices." Another easily interprets this as "I am a failure." When I point out every mistake my children make, I'm not only trying to control them in retrospect but I communicate, "You never get it right; you aren't good enough or trustworthy." Controlling is like a bowling ball to fragile crystal—devastating and shattering.

We damage ourselves with this approach as well. "I should be able to control our home, our family, our careers, and our universe," we unconsciously believe. The unfortunate companions of this belief are shame, because we frequently fail at the control panel, and stress, because our job is never done. What an exhausting way of life—much like trying to put out a raging forest fire by sprinkling it with a turkey baster. This basic attempt to put ourselves at the center of the world seems to be the root of our sin-sickness.

Other-Control

For some, life is a constant reaction to the actions of another. Someone makes us angry. We explode. Another's bad mood puts us in a bad mood. Someone changes the plans; we stay home or pout. Our students act rude; we act rude in return. When we allow another to determine our feelings and attitudes, we allow them to control us. It's no different than a teenager knuckling under to negative peer pressure. When we return evil for evil, ugly for ugly, we give up our own control and let others choose for us. We are out of control and cannot even control ourselves.

Self-Control

I prefer controlling others. It's more fruitful than controlling myself—my mouth, my actions, my thoughts. Mary laughed at this, saying, "I try to change the whole world, and I can't change myself." Maybe that's one of the reasons we try to control the world, because when we get down to it we can't rein ourselves in. When I'm concentrating on controlling another, I don't have to focus on my own failings and areas of improvement. I don't have to change, to go through painful soul-searching. I don't have to risk doing something wrong, because I'm so busy telling others how to do it right.

Self-control seems like a misnomer, an impossibility. Try as I might, I cannot get a grip on controlling myself by my own efforts.

But the Scriptures tell us that self-control is a hallmark of the Christian. Second Timothy 1:7 says we are not given a spirit of fear, but of love, of power, of self-control. Galatians says the fruit of the Spirit is self-control (5:22–23). I believe that is truly Spirit-control, which only works when I lean continually on God. Otherwise I'm pinning on my police badge at the least provocation, and I've again avoided reaching the roots of this control disease. The taproots of control sink deep into our souls.

Roots of Control

Too much of our striving, our busyness, and overcommitments is an effort to control the future, to manage or avoid processing the past, to buzz through the present without reflection. We attempt to manipulate another's impressions or opinions of us through our actions. Including, at times, God's opinions of us. Control IS our attempt at playing God, and it is rooted in fear.

The only way to get a grip on control is to open our hands. To let go. To replace our fear with its faith-filled opposite—trust.

Surrender

"I guess I really need to do what they say, 'Let go and let God,' " Debbie said.

Joanna laughed. "I hate that saying. I hate letting go of anything to *anybody*."

Isn't that the root of the control disease?

The only way out of the shaming cycle of control is to ask for help. To surrender. I have to say, "I cannot control my desire to control everyone and everything, and it's killing me and everyone I love." As we begin to recognize the insanity of our controlling, as the desire for freedom lurches and stumbles to life within us, we must realize that only God can restore us to sanity.

We must go outside of ourselves to find sanity. What irony that, as we give up control, we find it. As we die to our desire to run the world, we find new power. God's power. Spirit power. Real freedom lies in trusting God, in relinquishing.

The biggest problem with a chronic illness is that it is ongoing. The desire for control is chronic. A once-and-for-all conscious decision to relinquish our will and our lives into God's care is vital, but daily, even hourly or minute by minute, we must choose to wave the white flag. Former smokers who have given up the habit tell me, "Not a day goes by that I don't long for a cigarette." They must decide constantly to stay smoke-free. So is this sanity restoration ongoing, this continual handing over of the remote control to God.

Worry is about control, and control is about fear. About not trusting that God will take care of us. We think we are our own bottom line, but the truth is much greater: GOD is our bottom line. He has promised to be our keeper, the shade at our right hand. God has pledged to hold us in His palm and never forsake us. God has assured us that He acts in our own best interests, even when it doesn't look like that from our puny vantage point.

Living as if the spinning of the world depended upon us is living in complete denial of the life Christ surrendered for us that we might have life. Controllers continue to live by the Law (if I am good enough, if everything I do and everyone I know turns out well, then God will love and accept me). But Galatians 2:19–20 reads,

> For through the Law I died to the Law, that I might live to God. I have been crucified with Christ; and it is no longer I who live, but Christ lives in me; and the life which I now live in the flesh I live by faith in the Son of God, who loved me, and delivered Himself up for me.

Christ surrendered himself—His Godhood, His rights, His very life—first by veiling himself in human flesh, and second by giving all that up on the cross. When I continue to strive and control, I deny all that He has done for me and given up for me and stands waiting to do for me.

"Why do you do this, Jane?" Jesus asks tenderly. "I uphold the whole world. I care for your loved ones more than you dream possible. I'll take care of the outcome of everything you do. Loosen your grip. You don't have to clench them in the palm of your hand. I have them, securely, in my own palm."

In *Virtue* magazine, Jan Johnson, author of *Enjoying the Presence of God* (NavPress), writes,

> As we relinquish control and admit weaknesses, we remember who we are and why we're here. The sun does not rise and set on our achievements, but on the love of God. Life is a journey of coming to know God, not achieving or gaining others' approval. It's OK for us just to be and be and be, and love God. Through that being, God will do mightier works than when we try so hard.[2]

When we let go of fear and trust God, His faithfulness fills us and enables us to be faith-filled and faithful.

Hand It Over

I'm beginning to savor this relinquishment of the bit and bridle of control, to enjoy letting God steer. To quit anxiously scanning others' faces for reactions, to stop conniving ways to fix a situation or another's problems. I try to invite God to alert me before I control, or at the very least in the midst of a control war, so I can issue a cease-fire. Being still before the Lord, journaling, reflecting, or looking ahead—all of these help me to pay attention to control situations, like studying attack sites on the map in the war room.

Control is like work for me, and the complement of work is play. Play is more rooted in faith than anything else I do.

A giant oak tree in our yard stands resolute and firm, stern in its stripped, leafless state. Suspended from one of its mighty arms is a rope with a plank at the end for little bottoms. Daily the swing does its job—swinging!—propelled by our children and their friends. That swing represents something childlike and innocent, so playful and spontaneous. It sways in the winter wind, impudent and sassy. When Rich comes through the door, early from work, he asks, "Can I push you on the swing?"

I smile. A hundred to-dos rush through my head. I press *Save* on the computer, my smile widening, and take his hand.

And with the wind rushing through my hair, I grip the rope and sail high over the bluff, laughing, and know that I am beginning to heal.

Because if I can swing, I can play. And if I can play, I can trust. And trust is the end of controlling and the beginning of really living.

Quotes for Contemplation

Letting go does not mean to stop caring;
it means I can't do it for someone else.
Letting go is not to cut myself off;
it's the realization I can't control another.
Letting go is not to enable;
but to allow learning from natural consequences.
Letting go is to admit powerlessness;
which means the outcome is not in my hands.
Letting go is not to try to change
or blame another;
it's to make the most of myself.
Letting go is not to care for; but to care about.
Letting go is not to fix; but to be supportive.
It's not to judge but to allow another
to be a human being.
Letting go is not to be in the middle
arranging the outcome;
but to allow others to affect their
own destinies.
Letting go is not to be protective;
it's to permit another to face reality.
Letting go is not to deny; but to accept.
Letting go is not to nag, scold, or argue;
but to search out my own shortcomings
and correct them.
Letting go is not to adjust everything
to my desires;
but to take each day as it comes

and cherish myself in it.
Letting go is not to criticize
and regulate anybody;
but to try to become what I dream I can be.
Letting go is to not regret the past;
but to grow and live for the future.
Letting go is to fear less and live more.

—**AUTHOR UNKNOWN**

If you want to make God laugh, tell Him your plans.

—**A GRANDMOTHER**

The outworking of sin in various actions and thoughts is rooted in an essentially egocentric attitude, which impacts our relationship with our self, our God, and others. Sin is about controlling others, bending them to our desires, deflecting attention from our own failings. It's possible to love God and still struggle for control.

—**JANE RUBIETTA**

In my anxiety to conquer time by controlling its dispensation, I feel myself victimized by it. I am unable to find time, take time, get time: all control words. . . . But . . . when I imagine the simple way . . . there is AN AGENDA, and I'm in tune with it, but it's not my creation. I don't need to worry about controlling. . . . I'm not in command and I don't need to be. . . . Interruptions are as integral to the scene as anything I had planned. I only receive the day and the program that comes to me during the day from God. And that's what makes the difference.

—**ELAINE PREVALLET,**
AS QUOTED IN TOO DEEP FOR WORDS

As we become more aware of our controlling behavior . . . we stop manipulating situations in an effort to get our way. . . . As we begin to surrender our will and our lives to the care of God, we eliminate a great deal of stress and anxiety. We become willing to participate without being concerned about the outcome.

—**THE TWELVE STEPS—A WAY OUT**

So much of organized religion has been about control, stressing rules and regulations rather than a relationship. "To be acceptable, you must think, act, and look a certain way if you are a Christian." The message should be, "new in Christ" or "complete in Christ" or "filled to all the fullness of Christ."

—JANE RUBIETTA

Today, O Lord, I yield myself to you. . . . I place into your loving care my family, my friends, my future. Care for them with a care that I can never give. I release into your hands my need to control, my craving for status, my fear of obscurity.

—RICHARD FOSTER, AS QUOTED BY
JAN JOHNSON, AUTHOR OF
ENJOYING THE PRESENCE OF GOD

Letting go is both too simple and too difficult. It looks like weakness instead of strength, like losing instead of gaining, and it is. . . . Responding to God's call to surrender forces me to value my brokenness, as well as my strength.

—JAN JOHNSON,
"THE VIRTUE OF SURRENDER,"
VIRTUE

Scriptures *for* Meditation

For through the Law I died to the Law, that I might live to God. I have been crucified with Christ; and it is no longer I who live, but Christ lives in me; and the life which I now live in the flesh I live by faith in the Son of God, who loved me, and delivered Himself up for me.

—GALATIANS 2:19–20

Now listen, you who say, "Today or tomorrow we will go to this or that city, spend a year there, carry on business and make money." Why, you do not even know what will happen tomorrow. What is your life? You are a mist that appears for a little while and then vanishes. Instead, you ought to say, "If it is the Lord's will, we will live and do this or that."

—JAMES 4:13–15 NIV

A fool gives full vent to his anger, but a wise man keeps himself under control.

—PROVERBS 29:11 NIV

But the fruit of the spirit is love, joy, peace, patience, kindness, goodness, faithfulness, gentleness, self-control; against such things there is no law. Now those who belong to Christ Jesus have crucified the flesh with its passions and desires. If we live by the Spirit, let us also walk by the Spirit.

—**GALATIANS 5:22–25**

Finally, be strong in the Lord and in the strength of His might.

—**EPHESIANS 6:10**

I can do all things through Him who strengthens me.

—**PHILIPPIANS 4:13**

Journaling

Taking "inventory" of our day past, or looking to the day ahead, is a great way to fight the control war. Writing down a strategy of attack, or confessing with pen and paper where we've tried to control and facing the results, helps us realize the intensity of our grip on others.

Prayers of Confession, Praise, Petition

Prayer is sometimes another chance to try to control God: clarifying with Him our agenda, our desires, our goals. Instead of trying to tell God what to do, invite God to make clear to you His desires. Confession, praise, petition: all these, done with a whole heart, are examples of relaxing our grip and trusting God.

Moments for Creation

Trust is inherent in nature. Trees don't try to grow. Flowers don't try to bloom. They just do their job, and growth results. What other lessons might God be trying to impart as you observe the world He made?

Silence

Is there any time when we are less in control than when we wait silently in the presence of God? You might envision yourself actually handing over the thin, tattered reins of control, inviting Him to take the lead. Allow His reassuring love to wash over you and fill you as you wait.

Questions for Reflection

1. In what relationship do you most frequently experience the struggle to control? What means of control do you tend to use? Shame, anger, withdrawal?

2. What issues bring out your control disease? Which characteristics of control describe you?

3. How do you react to changes over which you have no control? To interruptions and unpleasant surprises? To what extent do you allow others to determine your reaction?

4. Take stock of the past week. What events or situations stand out in your mind as controlling moments for you? Where have you sensed God's advance warning system or help in the midst of controlling?

5. "Letting go," opening our clenched fist, seems ridiculous, even insane at times. But when we let go, we find that Someone greater has us in hand. When have you experienced this?

Hymn of Praise

I SURRENDER ALL

All to Jesus I surrender,
All to Him I freely give;
I will ever love and trust Him,
In His presence daily live.

REFRAIN:
I surrender all, I surrender all;
All to Thee, my blessed Savior,
I surrender all.

All to Jesus I surrender,
Make me, Savior, wholly Thine;
Let me feel the Holy Spirit—
Truly know that Thou art mine.

All to Jesus I surrender,
Lord, I give myself to Thee;
Fill me with Thy love and power,
Let Thy blessing fall on me.

—WORDS: JUDSON W. VANDEVENTER

CHAPTER EIGHT

Money, Money, Money: Money Means More Than We Think

Whether money makes us mad, manic, or moody, mammon packs a psychological and emotional wallop. Unpacking the meaning of money can change our lives.

The weak light splayed over my desk and my hunched shoulders, illuminating the stack of bills. The calculator's display reinforced the queasy feeling in my stomach, confirming what I already knew: We did not have the money to pay the bills. The nausea and the fear felt suffocating.

When I went to Rich with these facts, he came and looked dispassionately at the collection. Quickly he pointed out which ones to pay and which ones to hold, and advised me to bypass a savings deposit. "We'll be caught up in a month," he stated.

He was right. But his calm assessment of the situation contrasted dramatically with my own emotional and physiological reaction. Clearly Rich attaches a different emotional weight to money than I do.

I haven't finished the soul excavation necessary to understand my complex relationship with money. I'm not alone; money fuels more fights and raises more hackles between husbands and wives than nearly any other subject. Raise the subject of money, and church boards broil. Discuss raising taxes for educational needs, and citizens gird their loins for battle.

We've lost our perspective where money is concerned, obscuring its meaning in our daily lives, overlooking its powerful emotional hold.

One glance at a shopping mall confirms this. Women weighed down with shopping bags return home, after purchasing nothing they needed. A popular board game for girls involves the challenge of seeing who can spend all their money at the mall first. Garages, workbenches, rec rooms, kitchens, and makeup drawers reveal more widgets than stars in the sky.

With credit card debt at an all-time high, consumers max out all their plastic and then simply open a new credit card account, transferring existing balances to new accounts. Household debt for the average family now stands at ninety-three percent of annual disposable income.[1] Americans earn more than ever, yet gain less satisfaction from their money than at any time in the past. Bankruptcy appears to be an increasingly attractive way to get out of debt, keep most of the toys, and start over. In *Your Money or Your Life*, Jose Dominguez says we've gone from earning a living to earning a dying.[2]

Money is more than a matter of survival. It masters and motivates our lives.

Jesus mentioned money more often than any other subject; sixteen of his thirty-eight parables deal with money. Money matters. If we are to be faithful, we must deal with the meaning of money in our own lives, and answer the question "What are we trying to buy with our money?" The great mystique—and myth—of money is that it can purchase us safety, self-esteem, and power.

Money and Safety

Louise, born to a big family in the midst of the Great Depression years, had one drawer for her belongings and claimed the sofa as her bed. She remembers hunger and empty pockets and sitting in the car with her siblings while her father ate in a restaurant. Those feelings of deprivation and injustice haunted her, and throughout her work history, Louise devoted herself to her bosses, becoming invaluable to their success. Hard work ensured Louise not only money for necessities and luxuries but also a sense of safety and well-being.

Money purchased a measure of safety for Vera, too, as she gained national recognition for her sales and leadership abilities in a small but growing company. Money meant that she could support herself and her girls if her husband proved unfaithful; money also helped her feel good about her own abilities to take care of herself and her responsibilities.

The concept of using money or wealth to purchase safety is not new. In the Old Testament, the Israelites were frequently the target of surrounding countries, who were larger and wealthier than they. Often the Israelite kings, rather than rely on God's power and protection, taxed the people heavily and sent the tribute money to other countries, supposedly purchasing safety.

What they really secured, of course, was enslavement to the foreign rulers, the very thing from which the Lord had delivered them with great fanfare in Egypt.

With our devotion to buying, I wonder how different we are from the Israelites. Does our willingness to pay 18 to 20 percent interest demonstrate a slavish need for safety? What do our spending habits reveal about the depth of our spiritual/emotional poverty and lack of faith? And how much of our spending goes to purchase a better self-esteem?

Money, Self-Esteem, and Affection

In high school, every cent Diana earned baby-sitting went into her wardrobe. Fitting in with peers was essential to her self-esteem. Not much has changed. Women often use money to feel good about themselves, confusing net worth with self-worth. After a painful divorce, Lynda's department store credit card salved her misery. Whatever our age, it's easy to equate looking good with feeling valuable.

Jesus said, "Where your treasure is, there will your heart be also" (Luke 12:34). One woman with lovely, sculptured nails (upkeep: $50 per month, minimum) dropped a single dollar bill in the offering plate, making a strong statement about her values and sense of worth. Nothing wrong with sculptured nails: What we want to understand is what our spending habits reveal about our relationship with God and with ourselves.

Our ability to provide for loved ones also bolsters our sense of worth.

David found this to be true. As a child, his parents provided everything he wanted. Now as a father, he feels that cutting back because of a pinched budget denigrates his masculinity. In other words, real men—and women—provide for their families.

Underneath the love affair with money and buying hides the hope that money can, despite the Beatles' lyrics to the contrary, buy us love. And acceptance. Even adulation.

A story from Acts 8 demonstrates this. When Peter and John went to Samaria, they laid hands on people who had been baptized in the name of the Lord Jesus (v. 16). Converted to faith in Christ after a lucrative career in magic arts, Simon saw those people receive the Holy Spirit. He offered the apostles money, demanding, "Give this authority to me as well, so that everyone on whom I lay my hands may receive the Holy Spirit" (v. 19).

Peter's reply was swift and cutting: "May your silver perish with you, because you thought you could obtain the gift of God with money!" (v. 20).

After much admiration for his magic arts, Simon missed the power of the crowd's adulation and acceptance. Learning to find our worth, not in our income or what it can buy but in the imperishable love of God, is the only way we will ever find safety and acceptance.

Still, some surprising messages of power lurk in the lure of money.

Money and Power

When cheap became chic, the frugality wave of the '90s swept me under with its subtle message of power. Saving money meant that the advertising execs and their trickery did not sway me. Being thrifty—becoming master of what moolah we did have—nurtured the neurotic in me.

Frugality is always a trade off. Saving money steals time and energy from other priorities or responsibilities. Making meals from scratch, sewing our clothes, repairing our appliances: these appeal to my skinflint side and make me feel victorious over "the system." But frugality consumes large chunks of me, and I become preoccupied and even obsessive trying to buy less, save more, and make do. We are stewards of more than just our money; we must account for our time as well.

For most people, however, it's the flip side of money and power that is attractive. More money means more power. We can buy votes, offices, corporations. And let's face it, money solves a number of problems, such as hunger, medical care, housing, insurance. It's easy to assume money can also make us feel better about our losses, or buy us revenge if another has "done us wrong." This may be one reason that taking another to court is big business. Even so, a monetary settlement will not bring back a loved one lost to a drunken driver, or the use of a limb lost in a work-related accident. Nor will money erase grief, pain, or damaged emotions.

In light of the adulation of money's imaginary power, it's interesting to note that of all the commandments, the most overlooked one is "You shall not covet . . ." (Ex. 20:17). The Lord sternly reminds us, along with the wayward Israelites, not to envy our neighbor's spouse, slave, income—in fact, anything. We are not to covet anything belonging to another.

What a foreign concept in modern society. A television empire worth billions has built its foundation on coveting. The programs themselves are simply tools, designed to keep the viewer watching during the industry's *real* moneymakers, the commercial. And the commercials are geared to make us think that by spending a little (or a lot), we too can be beautiful, sporty, macho, popular, cool, rich, powerful. All this, and have white teeth, too.

Television is designed to make us want. And when we want, we take ourselves out of God's hand, as if He hasn't a clue about our needs and desires. Taking our eyes off Him as our Provider, we create fertile soil for the seeds of discontent.

Discontent

Our discontent—that desire for bigger, better, or different—should alert us to our tendency to use what is seen to medicate, numb, distract, or fill up. The temptation will always be to put people or power or possessions in the great gulf inside our souls, which can only be filled with God's presence.

This was behind God's warning in Deuteronomy 6:10–15. After their foray through the wilderness, the Israelites moved into homes they did not build, with wells they did not dig, and fields they did not till, plant, or tend. The Lord knew the human tendency to focus on possessions and forget the One who delivered it all to them. God rescued them from slavery, desiring to give them gifts, knowing full well the danger: that they would return to slavery by means of their possessions.

Jesus understood the danger of laying up treasures on earth, of worshiping our wallets or what our money (or plastic) can buy.

"Beware, and be on your guard against every form of greed; for not even when one has an abundance does his life consist of his possessions" (Luke 12:15). The temptation is twofold: to assume that life is what we see, and that we have brought it about in the first place.

Unlike the Israelites of the Old Testament, most of us are not farmers. Farmers know the intimate connection between God, the weather, and the harvest. When we non-agrarians receive a paycheck, we actually believe we earned it, rather than that God provided it for us. Our work is simply the conduit, the means by which God delivers our livelihood. When work or our employer acts as the middleman, we are easily blinded to our total dependence on the Lord. Knowing that God is ultimately responsible for us, we can hold our possessions lightly.

Money and an Eternity Mind-set

With God in charge of our well-being, we are free to live lives of deeper and great significance, creating ripple effects on into eternity. Cleo knows this. On her birthday, friends bought her a gift certificate for an appointment with a splashy stylist, who created a specially designed hairstyle. I saw Cleo days after her new 'do and raved over the flattering cut and the ease of care.

Cleo said, "I don't understand all this fuss over my hair. In ten years this haircut will mean nothing. That $150 could have helped keep three teenagers in a Christian rehab program for a month. Ten years from now the money spent on the teenagers would still be reaping benefits, and would continue reaping benefits until heaven. I don't want to put money on my head. I want to put it into heaven and people's hearts.

"I'm not going to upgrade my computer when the retired missionary is sitting on the floor in her empty apartment in an upper-class suburb with no income and no furniture and no food."

Weary of the drain on their time and income that caring for their large home induced, David and Lisa put their house on the market. It sold in one day, confirming their choice: "We're downsizing to free up more money and time for the kingdom."

Cleo, Lisa, and David have taken seriously the story Jesus told of the nobleman who gave his servants money, with the instructions to "put this money to work . . . until I come back" (Luke 19:13 NIV). This is unusual thinking in too many circles, but looking at money in terms of its effect on eternity sets us free. John Wesley said, "Earn all you can, save all you can, give all you can." When we give away our money, it no longer controls us.

Money and True Contentment

A glance at the spate of bills accumulating on my desk reminds me again of my own sporadic income and the unexpected expenses associated with being first-time homeowners. My stomach starts to clench, and my heart starts to pound in fear. The healing balm of trust spreads slowly. My mind knows that money, put in its proper place, no longer becomes a source of strength, safety, self-worth, or self-sufficiency, but my heart and faith are slow to comprehend this. The author of the letter to the Hebrews reminds me firmly, "Let your character be free from the love of money, being content with what you have; for He Himself has said, 'I will never desert you, nor will I ever forsake you' " (13:5).

With eternity in view, these bills are a reason for rejoicing in God's care, and the emotional, alluring, terrifying substance of mammon points me back to Christ.

Quotes for Contemplation

We are rich or poor according to what we are, not what we have.

—GEORGE MACDONALD,
DAVID ELGINBROD

To give away money is to win a victory over the dark powers that oppress us. [We must] reclaim for ourselves the energy with which we have endowed money: "Money is a hang-up for many of us. We will not be able to advance in the Christian faith until we have dealt at another level with the material [world]. It is a matter of understanding what it means to be faithful to Jesus Christ."

—ELIZABETH O'CONNOR,
QUOTING HER PASTOR,
FROM DEVOTIONAL CLASSICS
BY RICHARD FOSTER

Often people attempt to live their lives backward: they try to have more things, or more money, in order to do more of what they want so that they will be happier. The way it actually works is the reverse. You must first be *who you really are, then,* do *what you need to do, in order to* have *what you want.*

—**MARGARET YOUNG**

We make a living by what we get. We make a life by what we give.

—**WINSTON CHURCHILL**

But if thou art poor, then look not on thy purse when it is empty. He who desires more than God wills him to have, is also a servant of mammon, for he trusts in what God has made, and not in God Himself. He who laments what God has taken from him, he is a servant of mammon. He who for care cannot pray, is a servant of mammon.

—**GEORGE MACDONALD,
PAUL FABER, SURGEON**

We needed to make a conscious, daily decision to yield to God control of everything in our lives: our house, our cars, our clothes, our children—everything.

We realized that God wanted us to trust him alone to be our Provider. We had been trying to provide for ourselves—beyond our means—with credit. We . . . needed to learn to be content. . . . We had dishonored God's sovereignty and had denied his love when we used unsecured credit to buy bigger and better things for ourselves.

—**JEFF BERG,
"UNCONTROLLED SPENDING,"
DECISION MAGAZINE**

The rich man who held his things *lightly, nor let them nestle in his heart; who was a channel and no cistern; who was ever and always forsaking his money—starts, in the new world, side by side with the man who accepted, not hated, his poverty. Each will say, "I am free!"*

—**GEORGE MACDONALD,
UNSPOKEN SERMONS (SERIES TWO)**

Scriptures for Meditation

Do not wear yourself out to get rich; have the wisdom to show restraint. Cast but a glance at riches, and they are gone, for they will surely sprout wings and fly off to the sky like an eagle.

—**PROVERBS 23:4–5 NIV**

And now, O Israel, what does the Lord your God ask of you but to fear the Lord your God, to walk in all his ways, to love him, to serve the Lord your God with all your heart and with all your soul, and to observe the Lord's commands and decrees that I am giving you today for your own good? To the Lord your God belong the heavens, even the highest heavens, the earth and everything in it.

—DEUTERONOMY 10:12–14 NIV

Then it shall come about when the Lord your God brings you into the land which He swore to your fathers, Abraham, Isaac and Jacob, to give you, great and splendid cities which you did not build, and houses full of all good things which you did not fill, and hewn cisterns which you did not dig, vineyards and olive trees which you did not plant, and you shall eat and be satisfied, then watch yourself, lest you forget the Lord who brought you from the land of Egypt, out of the house of slavery. You shall fear only the Lord your God, and you shall worship Him, and swear by His name. You shall not follow other gods, any of the gods of the peoples who surround you, for the Lord your God in the midst of you is a jealous God.

—DEUTERONOMY 6:10–15

But godliness actually is a means of great gain, when accompanied by contentment. For we have brought nothing into the world, so we cannot take anything out of it either. And if we have food and covering, with these we shall be content.

But those who want to get rich fall into temptation and a snare and many foolish and harmful desires which plunge men into ruin and destruction. For the love of money is a root of all sorts of evil, and some by longing for it have wandered away from the faith, and pierced themselves with many a pang.

—1 TIMOTHY 6:6–10

Instruct those who are rich in this present world not to be conceited or to fix their hope on the uncertainty of riches, but on God, who richly supplies us with all things to enjoy. Instruct them to do good, to be rich in good works, to be generous and ready to share, storing up for themselves the treasure of a good foundation for the future, so that they may take hold of that which is life indeed.

—1 TIMOTHY 6:17–19

"Do not be afraid, little flock, for your Father has chosen gladly to give you the kingdom. Sell your possessions and give to charity; make yourselves purses which do not wear out, an unfailing treasure in heaven, where no thief comes near, nor moth destroys. For where your treasure is, there will your heart be also."

—LUKE 12:32–34

Journaling

In the safety of your journal, jot down your first thoughts about money and what emotional hold it might dangle over you.

Prayers of Confession, Praise, Petition

When we bring all the murky truths about ourselves and our feelings about money and safety and faith into the open, they weigh us down until we lay them at God's feet. Let this time of confession turn into praise as you find whole and complete forgiveness and acceptance in Christ.

Moments for Creation

In Matthew 6:28–29, Jesus bids us, "See how the lilies of the field grow. They do not labor or spin. Yet . . . not even Solomon in all his splendor was dressed like one of these" (NIV). As you spend time with God, notice how He provides for His creation. Where do you need to trust Him more for provisions in your own life?

Silence

After filling your heart with God's Word, invite the Holy Spirit to embrace you with a sense of God's presence. Let the silence encircle you, drawing you into the heart of God.

Questions for Reflection

1. What is your earliest memory of money? What messages did your parents give you about money? How have those early childhood lessons impacted your own view of money and its emotional power in your life?

2. What's on the material wish list you carry around in your heart? What do you secretly covet?

3. Where have you used money—or what it can buy—to feel good about yourself? To wield power, or control? To feel safe? To buy another's acceptance? Where has it supplanted God's presence and love in your life?

4. In what ways do you want to grow in relationship to money?

5. What changes would you like to make in the way you earn, spend, save, or give money? What is God leading you to do?

Hymn of Praise

I'D RATHER HAVE JESUS

I'd rather have Jesus than silver or gold,
I'd rather be His than have riches untold,
I'd rather have Jesus than houses or lands,
I'd rather be led by His nail-pierced hand
Than to be the king of a vast domain,
Or be held in sin's dread sway.
I'd rather have Jesus than anything
This world affords today.

I'd rather have Jesus than men's applause,
I'd rather be faithful to His dear cause,
I'd rather have Jesus than world-wide fame,
I'd rather be true to His holy name
Than to be the king of a vast domain,
Or be held in sin's dread sway.
I'd rather have Jesus than anything
This world affords today.

—**RHEA FLORENCE MILLER,**
GEORGE BEVERLY SHEA

CHAPTER NINE

Happy Hour: Finding Happiness in Everyday Life

We know we're to be joyful, and to be content in all circumstances, but we dole out happiness as if we lived on an emotional shoestring. Here we explore happiness as a by-product of the choices we make, the way we look at life, live our life, and give our life.

After arriving twenty-five minutes early for a meeting, I tooled down a side street to enjoy the landscaping and to decompress after a stressful day. Storms toyed with blue sky and sunshine. Suddenly, the sun painted a double rainbow, a slashing prism piercing the cloud's swollen darkness. I pulled back and forth to find the best view. The day's pressure evaporated in the presence of the masterpiece.

One homeowner's internal Neighborhood Watch beeped. He quit talking to his wife and started across the street toward me when I stopped. I grinned at his grimace and suspicious eyes, but still I watched the rainbow, knowing it would disappear in the blink of an eye.

"Can I help you?" he asked in anything but a helpful tone. My smile widened. I briefly met his eyes, then turned my gaze back to the sky. "No, thank you. I'm early for a meeting on the next street and wanted to watch the rainbow."

He turned, surprised, and walked toward the sky show. "Honey! Look at the sky!" he called, forgetting this threatening woman parked on his street and gathering wife and daughter to his side to see God's handiwork.

It was a brief moment, but the man changed from suspicious to happy simply by paying attention to that moment.

Happiness easily gets lost in the shuffle, like a small child in a crowd of adults. Suspicion crowds out beauty; anxiety elbows out contentment; stress takes up the disk space in our souls. We zoom through our days at high speed, too distracted by pressures and priorities and occasional paranoia to even recognize such a fleeting feeling. And while the Bill of Rights may claim happiness as an inalienable right, it's easy to confuse the pursuit of happiness with the purchase of possessions. The American Dream isn't about contentment as much as ownership. But possessions end up owning us, and we become consumed with their upkeep, focusing on managing the future or forgetting the past, and lose sight of the present moment.

And happiness exists only in the present moment.

Is Happiness Spiritual?

Doubt niggles. We shift uncomfortably when talking of happiness, as if happiness wasn't spiritual. Some of us grew up in circles that spoke reverently and seriously of "having a burden for such-and-such." This is good. The Lord does place burdens on our hearts, directing us to attend to certain matters or persons, but worriers are not deeper or more spiritual than happy people.

Along with burdens, the Lord places within us the capacity for happiness, for enjoying life. Hundreds of Scriptures reference joy, gladness, merriment, laughter. What else could the Lord mean in John 10:10, "I came that [you] might have life, and might have it abundantly"? Possessions and responsibilities become as thieves who break in and steal and destroy, but Jesus breaks through all that rusts, corrodes, and causes envy and says, "I came. . . ." Why give us the ability to feel a rush of pleasure over a butterfly, or the surge of laughter's healing burst at a child's antics, if not for use in the present? Heaven will be glorious beyond belief, but today is all we have right now. Tomorrow is up for grabs, but happiness ensures that we enjoy today.

We talk of joy in hushed, somber tones, but peeking back through time we see a king so overcome with joy that he danced in the streets. We see a God with such a sense of humor that He created frogs, and llamas with ludicrous lashes. We see Jesus, a man with a deep burden and a light heart, a heavy calling and a wacky sense of humor, trying to set us free from anxiety, to help us focus on the good. Imagine His playful smile when He described a camel squeezing through the eye of a needle.

When was the last time you danced with happiness? Laughed at a llama or giggled at a goose? Created a word picture that urged a smile?

We aren't talking about a self-centered, self-indulgent chasing of passionate excess. The pursuit of happiness can become an egotistical, me-first, me-always obsession, causing chaos and crisis at home and in the workplace. We don't expect to live on an emotional high, stuck on the "happy" setting. This smacks of denial! Normal is experiencing a broad range of emotions—but steady unhappiness is a sign that our focus is wrong; it is a choice to not be responsible for our own emotional well-being and represents a giving away of personal power.

Happiness Is a Powerbase

Blaming others for our unhappiness comes naturally, but truthfully, no one determines our emotions unless we give them the power. We give away power when we let people or circumstances decide our feelings. Betty fumes, "My mother makes me so mad. . . ." Or a wounded wife says, "He doesn't make me happy anymore," to justify her own unfaithfulness. As Father John Powell writes, "Growth begins where blaming ends."[1]

We also give away power when we try to make others responsible for our happiness. We might not say, "It's your fault I'm unhappy," but perhaps we live expecting others to create happiness for us. Blaming someone else is easier than taking responsibility for ourselves. Happiness is an individual choice, and while being in the presence of happy people may create feelings of happiness in us, others are not obligated to make us happy. Happiness cannot be externally based, dependent on others' actions or attitudes or attention. We alone are responsible for our happiness. As Father Powell says, "Happiness is an inside job."[2]

Nor does our job description include responsibility for another's happiness. We give away power when we try to control or arrange happiness in others; this is codependence. "If I can make you happy," we reason, "I will feel happy. Or at least safe." Or perhaps we try to control others in order to conform the world to our will, thinking that control equals happiness. Here again we forgo our chances for happiness.

Circumstantial evidence insists happiness is impossible. Jesus warned, "In the world you will have tribulation." But read on! He went on to say, "Be of good cheer! I have overcome the world" (John 16:33 NKJV). Happiness is possible and indestructible when based not on our circumstances or surroundings, but on truth: what we know to be true in Jesus Christ. Part of that truth is knowing and accepting who He created us to be.

Knowing Ourselves

A vague, undefined malaise settled over Carole. Her husband tried to prod and pry the problem from her. "What's wrong? What's making you unhappy? What do you want to be doing?" As he questioned her, Carole realized that part of her unhappiness was a lack of direction, created by not knowing her gifts or her strengths. After identifying her strong points and her dreams, she took charge of her own unhappiness by acting on those strengths and dreams. Too often we run the race we think others want us to run, rather than our own race. Pam Young and Peggy Jones write in *The Happiness File*,

> Your strengths are a key to your potential for happiness. They are gifts you were given, packed right into your little chromosomes. Your unique use of those God-given talents and attributes will provide you with everything you need to succeed in life.[3]

When we run the race God designed for us, happiness keeps pace with us in the form of contentment and joy. Embracing whom God created us to be empowers us to embrace life. Abundantly.

Barriers to Happiness

All this abundance aside, legitimate reasons exist for not feeling happiness. Either resolving the roadblocks or learning to live with those barriers enables us to find happiness.

We tend to focus on the most prominent, throbbing aspects of our lives. When those are negative, happiness is a stranger. For instance, grief, resentment, and unforgiveness barricade positive emotions, including happiness, by trapping us in the past. Because happiness is present tense, dwelling in past unhappiness blocks our growth. The only way past this blockade is to plow through the past, mourning appropriately, freeing another with forgiveness, and freeing ourselves of resentment.

Likewise, chronic pain may back us into an emotional corner, until we choose to find responsible and positive ways to refocus the pain. Addiction, too, whether our own or another's, blurs our vision, confusing us with a false world and a screwy definition of happiness. To the alcoholic or drug addict or even the romance novel junkie, happiness feels like the next high or binge or fantasy.

Lucy refused to adapt to life on her husband's farm, instead losing herself in soap operas and fictional romance. Her husband never measured up to Lucy's celluloid and paper heroes, and finally she left him. Another friend, Amanda, said, "If only my workaholic husband would straighten up, I'd be happy." This isn't happiness; it's wishful and deluded thinking.

Fatigue, an increasing problem among women today, dulls our wits and shadows our senses, making it hard to feel anything but exhaustion. We're tired but indispensable so we forge on, not realizing the push to get ahead actually undermines our hopes of happiness.

Comparison, too, destroys happiness—why else a special commandment for just this issue? "Thou shalt not covet your neighbor's . . ." anything! Whether we envy her new haircut or spontaneous nature or her big budget, comparison kills joy and contentment.

Finding Happiness

God fashioned us so that our parts interrelate, creating one harmonious whole; thus, our physical and spiritual states affect our emotional state. A good way to experience happiness is to prepare for it with a body that is properly fed and rested. You might try Jenn's theory: She loves jalapeños because they reputedly release a natural "drug" the body produces and thus elevate the mood. (Exercise also releases endorphins, for slightly more work, though both will make you sweat.)

Besides champing on hot peppers for a rush, multiple other methods engender happiness. All require a conscious choice, at least initially, to take the power given us to create happiness.

Happiness in the Present: Perspective

Annette, diagnosed with cancer and given less than a year to live, said, "This is the best year of my life. Every day, every moment is precious." By focusing not on her losses, not on her fear of the future, not on her pain, but on each moment as it presented itself, Annette learned a key to happiness: living each moment as if it were indeed her last.

We cannot afford the luxury of a negative thought. This is not denial. Tragedy is true. Great suffering and pain plague our world. But happiness exists as well. We have only to shift our gaze from the screaming headlines to the flower blooming defiantly on the deck. We needn't mourn with Job, "My eyes will never see happiness again" (7:7).

God can help us to be single-minded on the moment if we will only slow down and take time to see it. Richard Swenson said, "Life is a journey—not a race,"[4] and if we move too fast, we miss the scenery. Downshifting, we realize that the Creator of the heavens and the earth has the ultimate say-so in our lives and always has our best in mind.

Happiness in the Presence

Focusing, then, on God's presence in our midst—a miracle!—results in a lighter heart. Henri Nouwen said, "Joy and laughter are the gifts of living in the presence of God and trusting that tomorrow is not worth worrying about."[5]

A monk living in the seventeenth century found this secret to be true as well. Brother Lawrence learned to live with a constant awareness of God's love, deliberately turning thoughts and tasks into opportunities for conversation with God. "Thank you, Lord, for all nine hundred of these potatoes I have to peel" sort of opportunities. Sometimes we have to remember the facts of Faith 101: God specializes in redeeming even the worst of tasks or problems. The Lord knows our future, and it's a good one. "For I know the plans I have for you . . . plans to prosper you and not to harm you, plans to give you hope and a future" (Jer. 29:11 NIV). Such reviews give us a chance not only to rest in God's care of the future but also in His intimate interest in the dailyness of our lives.

Happiness and Praise

How can we not, then, bubble with praise? An unmistakable correlation exists between happiness and praise. Learning to praise God, even when we don't feel like it, changes our entire outlook. In the Old Testament, the Israelites rejoiced because they knew they were in good hands. Musical instruments, singing, and dancing frequently accompanied times of rejoicing. The earth shook with their praise. Music undoubtedly enhances moods and has even been associated with physical and emotional healing.[6]

Laughter brings healing as well, as Norman Cousins demonstrated in *Anatomy of an Illness*. Shortly after a difficult period in our family, when Rich and I dropped in on a meeting, laughter prevailed more than business. Though I barely knew the others, I laughed along with them. Later, noticing a strange lightness of soul, I recognized the healing work of spontaneous laughter throughout the evening. I hadn't realized how rarely we laughed through the preceding season. Solomon knew the value of laughter all along when he said, "A merry heart doeth good like medicine" (Prov. 17:22 KJV). Laughter and praise can save your life, make your day, and change your priorities.

Happiness and Giving

Helping others also shifts our focus. Albert Schweitzer said, "I don't know what your destiny will be, but one thing I know: the only ones among you who will be really happy are those who will have sought and found how to serve."

Rather than focusing on her disappointments and pain, Liz went back to school after losing her sight, and now with a psychology degree volunteers at the local hospital. Her blindness, she says, "restored her vision" for serving others.

Of course, this can result in more items on our to-do list, more pressure and responsibility, and we must guard our commitments and carefully examine our priorities. But happiness becomes a selfish pursuit when we think exclusively of ourselves.

Belly Up

The sense of fullness, of abundance, of contentment silvered with flashes of joy—this is happiness. Being open to the present, tuning in to our senses and our reactions: these help us notice happiness when it comes near. It's easier to moan with Eeyore, "Looks like rain," than to use silver-lining thinking, but when we consciously look for the good, our lives change, worry furrows fade, and happiness invades our personal space.

Maybe we should beat out the local bars and call our time with the Lord a "happy hour," a time when we belly up to the banquet table of God's delights, when we indulge in a feast time of gratitude and praise, of silence, journaling, feeding on Scripture, drinking from the fountain of God's love.

So go ahead, friends. Belly up, and, as they say, "Bottoms up!" Drinks are on the House, and it's a bottomless cup.

Quotes for Contemplation

Joy is essential to spiritual life. Whatever we may think or say about God, when we are not joyful, our thoughts and words cannot bear fruit. . . . I remember the most painful times of my life as times in which I became aware of a spiritual reality much larger than myself, a reality that allowed me to live the pain with hope. I dare even to say, "My grief was the place where I found my joy. . . ." We have to choose joy and keep choosing it every day. It is a choice based on the knowledge that we belong to God and have found in God our refuge and our safety and that nothing, not even death, can take God away from us.

**—HENRI NOUWEN,
HERE AND NOW:
LIVING IN THE SPIRIT**

We thank Thee, Lord, for the glory of the late days and the excellent face of Thy sun. We thank Thee for good news received. We thank Thee for the pleasures we have enjoyed and for those we have been able to confer. And now, when the clouds gather and rain impends over the forest and our house, permit us not to be cast down; let us not lose the savor of past mercies and past pleasures; but, like the voice of a bird singing in the rain, let grateful memory survive in the hour of darkness.

—ROBERT LOUIS STEVENSON

To live fully, outwardly and inwardly, not to ignore the external reality for the sake of the inner life, or the reverse—that's quite a task.

—ETTY HILLESUM

Happiness Makes Up in Height for What It Lacks in Length.

**—ROBERT FROST,
1942, TITLE OF A POEM**

I am convinced that happiness is within the reach of everyone. The only problem is that if we reach out, we are going in the wrong direction. Happiness is, and has always been, an inside job. . . . Happiness is also a by-product. It is the result of doing something else. . . . Happiness cannot be directly pursued.

—JOHN POWELL,
HAPPINESS IS AN INSIDE JOB

Always leave enough time in your life to do something that makes you happy, satisfied, even joyous. That has more of an effect on economic well-being than any other single factor.

—PAUL HAWKEN,
QUOTED IN THE ARTIST'S WAY

Everyone will be called to account for all the legitimate pleasures which he or she has failed to enjoy.

—THE TALMUD

Happiness that the world cannot take away only flourishes in the secret garden of our souls. By tending to our inner garden and uprooting the weeds of external expectations, we can nurture our authentic happiness the way we would nurture something that's beautiful and alive. Happiness is a living emotion . . . *not a frivolous, expendable luxury.*

—SARAH BAN BREATHNACH,
SIMPLE ABUNDANCE: A DAYBOOK OF COMFORT AND JOY

Scriptures for Meditation

An anxious heart weighs a man down, but a kind word cheers him up.

—PROVERBS 12:25 NIV

"Therefore you too now have sorrow; but I will see you again, and your heart will rejoice, and no one takes your joy away from you. . . . Until now you have asked for nothing in my name; ask, and you will receive, that your joy may be made full. . . . These things I have spoken to you, that in Me you may have peace. In the world you have tribulation, but take courage; I have overcome the world."

—JOHN 16:22, 24, 33

Blessed be the God and Father of our Lord Jesus Christ, who according to His great mercy has caused us to be born again to a living hope through the resurrection of Jesus Christ from the dead. . . . Though you have not seen Him, you love Him, and though you do not see Him now, but believe in Him, you greatly rejoice with joy inexpressible and full of glory, obtaining as the outcome of your faith the salvation of your souls.

—1 PETER 1:3, 8–9

The fruit of the Spirit is love, joy, peace, patience, kindness, goodness, faithfulness, gentleness, self-control; against such things there is no law.

—GALATIANS 5:22–23

I have set the Lord continually before me;
because He is at my right hand, I will not be shaken.
Therefore my heart is glad, and my glory rejoices;
My flesh also will dwell securely.
For Thou wilt not abandon my soul to Sheol;
Neither wilt Thou allow Thy Holy One to undergo decay.
Thou wilt make known to me the path of life;
In Thy presence is fullness of joy;
In Thy right hand are pleasures forever.

—PSALM 16:8–11

Let all who take refuge in Thee be glad,
Let them ever sing for joy;
And mayest Thou shelter them,
That those who love Thy name may exult in Thee.
For it is Thou who dost bless the righteous man, O Lord,
Thou dost surround him with favor as with a shield.

—PSALM 5:11–12

A happy heart makes the face cheerful,
but heartache crushes the spirit.

—PROVERBS 15:13 NIV

Now may the God of hope fill you with all joy and peace in believing, that you may abound in hope by the power of the Holy Spirit.

—ROMANS 15:13

Journaling

Consider the question "What makes you happy?" and spend some time journaling your response. Try to write without deep thought—the first things that come to mind. This needn't elicit super-spiritual responses, although those are fine too. Just grab your honest answers before the editor within axes them.

Prayers of Confession, Praise, Petition

Turning our hearts toward God is not a movement of anxiety but one of grace. Dare to draw near to the throne of grace, that you may receive mercy and may find grace to help in time of need (Heb. 4:16).

Moments for Creation

How about focusing on one of your senses while outside today? Stop in your meanderings, close your eyes, and breathe deeply. Smell the pine trees, the spring blossoms, the honeysuckle, the autumn leaves, the crisp snowy air. . . . Whatever the season, let the incredible sense of smell inform you. What a God, to create such variety—just for our *noses*!

Silence

Breathe deeply in the silence. Inhale God's grace; exhale any sense of failure, the unhappy clutter of your thoughts. Breathe in again, slowly, focusing on the presence of God. Allow the Holy Spirit to fill you, to inform you, to bring you to a place of deep rest in Christ.

Questions for Reflection

1. What are some of your happiest memories? How do you feel about happiness? Are you a happy person? How often do you feel happy? Have there been seasons in your life that were happier than others? What about this season?

2. Of the barriers to happiness mentioned, with which do you struggle the most: unforgiveness, resentment, fatigue, chronic pain, loss, addiction, comparison? You might consider keeping a thankful journal, listing all you have to be thankful for.

3. When do you feel happy? What makes you happy? How often do you allow yourself the treat of deliberately putting yourself in the path of happiness (i.e., choosing an activity solely because it will be fun)? Whose race are you running?

4. When have you experienced joy in serving another? Or felt torn between helping others in order to feel good about yourself and serving out of a sense of your fullness?

5. In what ways might God be leading you into happiness right now? What changes would you need to make in your life to experience more joy?

Hymn of Praise

To God Be the Glory

To God be the glory, great things He hath done;
So loved He the world that He gave us His Son,
Who yielded His life an atonement for sin,
And opened the life gate that all may go in.

Refrain:
Praise the Lord, praise the Lord,
Let the earth hear His voice!
Praise the Lord, praise the Lord,
Let the people rejoice!
O come to the Father through Jesus the Son,
And give Him the glory, great things He hath done.

O perfect redemption, the purchase of blood,
To every believer the promise of God;
The vilest offender who truly believes,
That moment from Jesus a pardon receives.

Great things He hath taught us, great things He hath done,
And great our rejoicing thro' Jesus the Son;
But purer, and higher, and greater will be
Our wonder, our transport, when Jesus we see.

—**FANNY CROSBY**

CHAPTER TEN

Don't Let the Bedbugs Bite: Working on Worry and Fret

Worry is the acceptable kin to fear, though more invasive and insidious and pervasive. We worry without even thinking about it! We dress it up and call it anxiety, but worry is a thief, longing to steal our very vitality. How can we be free from the slavish demands of worry and be able to embrace the potential in each day?

Birds flutter over the wedding's remnants, gobbling up dry rice greedily, as if there were no tomorrow, as if they aren't sure the heavenly platter will deliver the next portion, as if there aren't enough bugs and worms and grain to go around. But it is believed the rice soaks up the moisture in the birds' tiny tummies, swelling them to capacity, and the birds die of either constipation or a burst stomach.

Worries are like that—we hoard them greedily, knowing tomorrow is uncertain and suspecting that we are the only ones able to carry these things. Worries swell in the soul like rice in a bird's stomach, and now, settling before God in the quiet, after my worry binge, I long to purge—to spew up all the anxiety I have so carelessly, thoughtlessly swallowed in fits of self-centeredness and self-sufficiency.

We clutch worry to our breasts, nurse it like infants, bind it to us like the Israelites bound God's Word to their foreheads. We eat, breathe, and forgo sleep for worry. This simple bedtime ditty, meant to provide comfort to us as children, gives grist for the worry mill as adults.

Now I lay me down to sleep,
I pray the Lord my soul to keep.
If I should die before I wake,
I pray the Lord my soul to take.

"What if I DO die in my sleep? What about the children? Did I make a will? Ought I change it? And will the Lord really take my soul? I wonder who would find me dead in my bed? I don't want it to be my kids. And the house is such a mess. I should pay that bill, and get some groceries. . . ."

At nighttime, the bedbugs DO bite, and their names are Worry and Fret.

What Is Worry?

The *Oxford English Dictionary* defines worry "to strangle, throttle, kill by violence . . . to seize by the throat and tear or lacerate, e.g., dogs or wolves attacking sheep." When Jesus visits Mary and Martha, Martha is "worried and distracted by many things" (Luke 10:38–42 NRSV). Here the word distracted means "dragged around by her worries."

Many of us can relate. Worry drags us through our days like ants drag food to their hills. Whether we are hand-wringers or rut-in-the-rug worriers or one of the 25 percent of Americans who will suffer from an anxiety disorder, worry wastes time, energy, and potential. It can wreck our workday, our homelife, our health. Dr. Charles Mayo, of the Mayo Clinic, says, "Worry affects circulation, the glands, the whole nervous system, and profoundly affects the heart." Worry can kill us. Even if worry isn't fatal for us, Edward M. Hallowell, M.D., writes in his book *Worry: Controlling It and Using It Wisely*,

> Excessive worry is an exhausting and dangerous problem for millions of Americans. People who worry a lot *suffer*, as do the people close to them. . . . A recent survey of primary care physicians in the United States reported that at least *one-third* of office visits were prompted by some form of anxiety. Furthermore, over the course of a lifetime, at least one in four people—65 million individuals—will meet the criteria for one or more of the medical conditions called "anxiety disorders," treatable disorders defined by the presence of debilitating worry.[1]

If you suspect you may have one of the five main anxiety disorders—panic disorders, phobias, obsessive-compulsive disorder, post-traumatic stress, or generalized anxiety—please consult your physician. But whether we are chronic worriers or simply "concerned" or "thinking out loud," we worry naturally. A Rubietta Informal Poll reveals our worries.

Worrisome Subjects

Around the circle, men and women alike clustered their worries. My instructions to the group were: "Without thinking about it, share the very first worry that comes to your mind." Some said, "I'm not worried, I'm concerned," which we immediately waved aside as prettified anxiety. Regardless of age, the subjects of worry could generally be grouped into three categories: money, health, and loved ones. Often these concerns overlapped.

For the widows, financial and health concerns linked arms: How long can I live independently? All parents, regardless of their child's age, mentioned anxiety over offspring. Cleo, nearing retirement, had just met with a financial adviser and wondered, "How much is enough?" (Because money is a matter over which many of us are concerned, more attention was given this anxiety in chapter 8.)

Regardless of the subject of our worries, humans are wired for worry.

Why We Worry

Physiological reasons exist for worry, as well as "negative benefits" derived from this brain drain. Dr. Hallowell writes,

> Fear and its complex descendant, worry, rise up within us as naturally as hunger or thirst. Hormones, nerve cells, neurotransmitters, great chunks of the brain, sensors in the skin, reflex arcs, involuntary muscles, even hearts—all these stand on alert twenty-four hours a day, seven days a week, poised to make us feel fear and act upon it.[2]

And because we've confused fear with worry in our minds for so long, the worry path is well-worn in our brains. Strictly speaking, only rare times warrant genuine fear, because fear is legitimate only when the logical outcome of the event feared is pain or death.[3] Legitimate fear can save our lives; worthless worry can kill us. Do you ever groan, "She's about to worry me to death"? That may be closer to the truth than we like to admit.

Ultimately worry must reward us in some way for us to continue the destructive habit.

Complex Benefits

B. F. Skinner taught, "All behavior has meaning," so in the case of worry, it's important to ask ourselves what we are getting from anxiety. What "negative" benefits does worry bring?

- Worry diverts our attention, helping us avoid dealing with past pain or trauma by occupying our minds with other, smaller things. Marcel Proust said, "We are healed of a suffering only by experiencing it to the full." Until we give ourselves permission to heal, insignificant worries may overwhelm us.
- Worry distracts us from listening to our dreams, from taking risks, from heeding our calling. In a perverse way, worry protects us from risk.
- Worry keeps us from having to change, because when we worry, we don't do anything about the object of worry.
- Worry substitutes for action, since we feel like we're accomplishing something through worry.
- Worry busies brain cells with the worst-case scenario, protecting us from disappointment or shock should it actually happen.

In short, worry wastes our potential, unless we allow anxiety to instruct us.

Worry Lessons

Though worry can drastically affect our well-being, it does teach us some positive points.

- Worry can show us our vulnerabilities. "I'm worried I won't get the job," Helen frets, then asks herself, "Where do I need to grow professionally in order to move up to that position?" By checking out her worries, she can strengthen her weak points.
- Worry can help us see disadvantages and work around them.
- Worry can increase our performance. Speakers welcome butterflies, which edge their talks with urgency. Beyond a certain level of worry, though, our performance level drops.
- Worry can reveal to us where we aren't trusting God. As a signpost, worry always directs us back to the heart of God.

The Word on Worry

Being told not to worry is like being told not to breathe. Worry comes naturally—an almost involuntary response that we don't even think about. And yet we are admonished in Scripture NOT to worry. "Be anxious for nothing," orders Paul (Phil. 4:6). In fact, we're constantly asked to do the unnatural. How? Do fish walk? Do turtles sing?

Yet here's the most amazing part of the admonitions in Scripture: We don't need to OWN these problems, to carry them. We're not just told, like some inane song, "Don't worry, be happy," but we are *always* directed to the *One* who can handle our cares. "Do not be anxious . . . for your heavenly Father knows that you need all these things" (Matt. 6:31–32) and "My God shall supply all your needs . . . in *Christ Jesus*" (Phil. 4:19). We are always pointed to the author and *perfecter* of our faith. *We* don't perfect our faith, cleaning up our act, getting ourselves in order so we don't worry. That would be idolatry: trusting in ourselves again. No, it is Jesus who perfects our faith.

We tangle our feet in the temporary. And Jesus says, "Life isn't made up of what we own! Don't worry about what you'll wear or what you'll eat! God knows what you need!" (Luke 12:15, paraphrase). We make the mistake of believing that life is what we see, but what we see is only the tip of the iceberg. We focus on the physical details of life—money, food, clothes, house—and forget that these needs are tools that point us back to God, to trust His love and provision for us.

Because worry wears a track in our brain that gets easier to use the more we run down it, we need to learn to control worry before we ever start the train.

Controlling Worry

Stop Stoking the Boiler: Recognizing Worry

The first and most likely step to dealing with anxiety is to recognize it. Because worry requires no conscious effort, before we know it we're on the train and moving down the track. Our thoughts feed the process like wood stokes a boiler. Tuning in to that thought process, that stoking, is key. Beginning to recognize the early stages of worry—the hunched shoulders or pinched brow, the pacing or the nervous chatter—alerts us to the problem. "Whoa," we say, "what's this about? What's happening here?" In this way, we stop stoking the boiler before the train races down the rails.

Switching Tracks: Rerouting Worry

A second means of halting the train is by rerouting it. We CHOOSE which rail to ride: the Anxiety Express or the Freedom Train. The worry track always ends up with the worst-case scenario; the freedom train delivers us to a place of safety and trust. Therapists who treat long-term depression, as well as those who deal with anxiety, tell us we can retrain the neurotransmitters that convey worry messages to our brain by changing our thought patterns. Getting ourselves to switch tracks, jumping off the "stinkin' thinkin' " train, changing our perspective, is much easier when we make the right connections.

Confession Connections

The most commonplace, therapeutic receptacle for worry is connection: connection with ourselves, with others, and with God. Unfortunately, few of us listen to our lives. For some of us, worry begins as a tiny, flying pebble and spreads like spider-web cracks on a windshield. Some of us worry exponentially, moving from "Her plane is ten minutes late" to "They'll drop the coffin at her funeral" in a nanosecond. Or maybe you're like Alice's aunt, who flips a positive into a negative in one sentence. "It's sunny out" becomes "Don't get heatstroke!" Or, "Today's going to be chilly" dramatically leads to "You'll have to get your toes amputated because of frostbite and you'll never be a dancer."

We connect with ourselves when we look up from the frenzied pacing of our souls and ask, "What am I fretting about?" When I realize I'm carrying tomorrow's worries today, I pull out my journal and pour out the troubles. The journal once again becomes a confessional, a safe place where I can agonize in ink, emptying my brain of worry.

Once we identify the bees swarming in the hive of our minds, it's easier to connect with God and others, because we've located the troubles. Whereas our worries actually separate us from loved ones and God, when we share them, the load lightens, and we are brought closer. We may be wired for worry, but we are also made for relationships. And the most significant relationship of our lives is with One who longs to carry our worries for us.

Sometimes, however, the connections we make contribute to our worries. After an emergency room visit, Jenna worried about her family health history and began jogging and watching her weight and cholesterol. She subscribed to a "natural" remedy magazine exploring every imaginable problem—and some she hadn't imagined. After each issue arrived, Jenna headed to the health food store to ward off a new problem, occupied with worry. Finally, Jenna's husband tired of the paranoia and halted the subscription. She didn't need new health alerts to feed her worry.

The widows in a retirement community phoned one another regularly, discussing deaths, surgeries, aches, and pains. It's good to connect, but relationships should feed the positive. Hanging around pessimistic peers will not help your worries. Neither will the news media.

Worry is the passion of the news moguls. They specialize in creating anxiety, whether over poisoning in our fresh veggies or highway shootings. We respond like frenzied sharks feeding on bloody bait. One friend canceled her newspapers and refuses to watch the local news. "I have enough to worry about without hearing about e-coli," she says. "The more we know, the more we worry."

Creative Rerouting

An important part of treatment of worry is to change basic habits: exercise, sleep, proper diet, abstinence from alcohol. Such simple changes profoundly impact the worry engine. Changing the way we live and look at our lives will derail worry.

Another switch track for the worry train is creative rerouting. Worries begin in the imagination, where dreams also begin. Worriers employ creativity negatively. They peer ahead and imagine the worst. Mark Twain said, "I have had a great many troubles, but most of them never happened." Creative rerouting turns away from the worst and begins to imagine the best outcomes.

Gavin DeBecker, who built a career by helping people track their fears and distinguish legitimate fear from worry, writes,

> The history of invention is filled with perceived failures that became unpredicted successes. . . . I have gotten great benefits from taking the voice of skepticism that I used to apply to my intuition and applying it instead to the dreaded outcomes I imagined were coming. Worry will almost always buckle under a vigorous interrogation. If you can . . . apply your imagination to finding the possible favorable outcomes of undesired developments, even if only as an exercise. You'll see that it fosters creativity.[4]

Perhaps the most creative way to confound worry and redirect the beast is through blessing. (I hate this one, but it really works.) After trying to confess, to trust God, to look at the possible creative outcomes of a worrisome subject, only one thing remains: to give thanks. Paul's injunction, "Be anxious for nothing!" doesn't stop there. Such an order is fruitless. He continues with a remedy: "But in everything, with prayer and *thanksgiving*, let your requests be made known to God" (Phil. 4:6).

Thank God? That, for instance, we're driving a rusty heap of metal, worrying with each trip about safety and repair bills? No. I don't think Scripture tells us to thank God for the problem itself, but to thank Him for His faithfulness to care for us, for His presence in the midst of trial, for His permanence in our lives. When I'm chagrined over the iron oxide chewing up my car, or tempted to betray my anti-loan beliefs and borrow money for payments, or embarrassed because driving such a car looks like I'm a starving artist (not far from the truth), I remember: this car was a gift! (Thank you, Lord!) This green-gilled dinosaur has taken us 100,000 miles! (Thank you, Lord!) Driving this car helps us save money! (Thank you, Lord!) Driving this car keeps me humble (Well . . .). Putting thousands of miles on my '81 wagon while driving to speaking engagements is much smarter than running the tread off the tires of a new car (Yes, God!).

And quickly my heart turns to praise for the ways God has provided for us, keeping us safe and holding our good at the center of His heart. I can thank the Lord for His timing, trusting Him for the future, knowing that He is far more concerned about our welfare and that of our loved ones than we even have the sense to be. Better than a feeding frenzy on anxiety, try feeding on God's overwhelming compassion for us.

The result? "And the *peace of God*, which transcends all understanding, will guard your hearts and your minds in Christ Jesus" (Phil. 4:7 NIV).

Quotes for Contemplation

God is nearer to you than any thought or feeling of yours. . . . Do not be afraid. If all the evil things in the universe were around us, they could not come inside the ring that He makes around us. He always keeps a place for Himself and His child, into which no other being can enter.

—**GEORGE MACDONALD,**
DAVID ELGINBROD

Too much worry leads to a host of medical complications, from depressed immune function, to heart disease, to gastrointestinal disorders of all kinds, to an array of different types of headaches and musculoskeletal pains about the body. It has even been found that anxiety disorders in adolescent girls can result in stunted growth! Furthermore, excess worry impairs judgment, induces fatigue, increases irritability, and in general makes a person a less effective leader or worker. You need to learn to worry well so that worry does not become destructive, consuming you instead of arming and alarming you as it should.

—**EDWARD M. HALLOWELL, M.D.,**
WORRY: CONTROLLING IT AND USING IT WISELY

Applying logic to anxiety was like trying to reason with a swarm of bees.

—**TRACY THOMPSON,**
THE BEAST

Like an ant on a stick,
both ends of which are burning,
I go to and fro without knowing
what to do, and in great despair.
Like the inescapable shadow that
follows me, the dead weight of sin
haunts me.

Graciously look upon me.
Thy love is my refuge.

—**TRAD., INDIA**
AS QUOTED IN THE UNITED METHODIST HYMNAL

The next hour, the next moment, is as much beyond our grasp and as much in God's care, as that a hundred years away. Care for the next minute is just as foolish as care for the morrow, or for a day in the next thousand years—in neither can we do anything, in both God is doing everything. Those claims only of the morrow which have to be prepared to-day are of the duty of to-day; the moment which coincides with work to be done, is the moment to be minded; the next is nowhere till God has made it.

—**GEORGE MACDONALD,**
UNSPOKEN SERMONS (SERIES III)

When we root ourselves in reality—that Jesus is the same yesterday, today, and forever, that God never changes, and will never leave us or forsake us—our worries erode like sand in the outgoing tide, leaving us resting on solid Rock. God truly becomes our restingplace, where our fears and worries can rest, taken up by the One who knows our future. "For I know the plans that I have for you, plans for welfare and not for calamity, to give you a future and a hope."

—**JANE RUBIETTA**

Worrying is carrying tomorrow's load with today's strength—carrying two days at once. It is moving into tomorrow ahead of time. Worrying does not empty tomorrow of its sorrow—it empties today of its strength.

—**CORRIE TEN BOOM,**
HE CARES, HE COMFORTS

Scriptures for Meditation

"Therefore I tell you, do not worry about your life, what you will eat; or about your body, what you will wear. Life is more than food, and the body more than clothes. . . . Who of you by worrying can add a single hour to his life? Since you cannot do this very little thing, why do you worry about the rest? . . . And do not set your heart on what you will eat or

drink; do not worry about it. For the pagan world runs after all such things, and your Father knows that you need them. But seek his kingdom, and these things will be given to you as well. Do not be afraid, little flock, for your Father has been pleased to give you the kingdom."

—LUKE 12:22–23, 25–26, 29–32 NIV

Be anxious for nothing, but in everything by prayer and supplication with thanksgiving let your requests be made known to God. And the peace of God, which surpasses all comprehension, shall guard your hearts and your minds in Christ Jesus.

Finally . . . whatever is honorable, whatever is right, whatever is pure, whatever is lovely, whatever is of good repute, if there is any excellence and if anything worthy of praise, let your mind dwell on these things.

—PHILIPPIANS 4:6–8

For I know the plans I have for you . . . plans to prosper you and not to harm you, plans to give you hope and a future.

—JEREMIAH 29:11 NIV

Humble yourselves, therefore, under the mighty hand of God, that He may exalt you at the proper time, casting all your anxiety upon Him, because He cares for you.

—1 PETER 5:6–7

Journaling

Pull out your journal, and pour out your anxious thoughts (Ps. 139:23–24). Anxiety nibbles around the edges of our minds like mice around paper, but if we put it outside our minds, we remove some of its power.

Prayers of Confession, Praise, Petition

Because worry is actually a way of trying to control the future, confession may be the next logical step in the process of eliminating fret. Knowing that God is faithful to forgive, we're free from anxiety to praise Him and to bring those petitions to Him.

Moments for Creation

"Observe how the lilies of the field grow; they do not toil nor do they spin, yet . . . even Solomon in all his glory did not clothe himself like one of these" (Matt. 6:28–29). Indeed, examining the great care God took with creation should relieve our hearts about our own place in His care. Today, as you walk, turn your eyes to observe that beauty and apply it to your life, for "Are you not worth much more than they?" (Matt. 6:26).

Silence

Let the Word of God fill your mind and soul, then practice casting your cares on God. Release them, and let the peace of God surround you. Listen, focusing only on the Lord. "My soul, wait in silence for God only."

Questions for Reflection

1. Without stopping to analyze your answer, quickly write down your biggest worry. Even if you are not a chronic worrier, do you tend to focus on one area of your life, or one person? What else worries you?

2. I didn't think I worried until one morning my dreams awakened me at 4:00 A.M., graphically revealing that I was very worried. How does worry show up in you? Sleeplessness? Dreams? Constant movement? Poor health habits? Smoking, pacing, eating?

3. Is there a pattern of worry in your parents? Sometimes worriers are genetically wired for worry. Where can you seek help for your worries? Who feeds your worries? What sorts of connections have you made?

4. What is your natural response when a worry springs upon you? When have your worries thrown you upon Christ, and resulted in a blessing?

5. The word "casting" in 1 Peter 5:6–7 actually means "hurling." Ask God to reveal the things you are worried about. Imagine hurling those things into God's capable catcher's hands! How do you feel, knowing that God is concerned about the things that concern you?

Hymn of Praise

BE STILL, MY SOUL

Be still, my soul: the Lord is on your side.
Bear patiently the cross of grief or pain;
leave to your God to order and provide;
in every change God faithful will remain.
Be still, my soul: your best, your heavenly friend
through thorny ways leads to a joyful end.

Be still, my soul: your God will undertake
to guide the future, as in ages past.
Your hope, your confidence let nothing shake;
all now mysterious shall be bright at last.
Be still, my soul: the waves and winds still know
the Christ who ruled them while he dwelt below.

Be still, my soul: the hour is hastening on
when we shall be forever with the Lord,
when disappointment, grief, and fear are gone,
sorrow forgot, love's purest joys restored.
Be still, my soul: when change and tears are past,
all safe and blessed we shall meet at last.

—WORDS: KATHARINA VON SCHLEGEL, 1752

CHAPTER ELEVEN

The Hospitable Heart

Real hospitality goes beyond rugs and wreaths and wall decor; true hospitality is found in the heart of God. Though it is costly, when we find our home in God, we can open our homes to others.

Home wasn't fancy and was small by many standards today. The welcome lay not in the furbishings but in the attitude that cloaked my parents' home: *You are important*. Anyone was welcomed, brought inside: childhood friends, cast-off boyfriends, the traveler needing a bed, a college buddy snoozing in the hammock while waiting for us. There were frequent youth group gatherings and friends over to study, play euchre, or fit together a puzzle. One friend, Nancy, let herself in; when we returned, a pecan pie bubbled in the oven. Laughter and welcome abounded in our home when the door was open, and the storm door was rarely shut. Shoes, toed-off at door and hearth, signaled the presence of a constant parade of people, young and old, testifying to their at-homeness.

A longing has begun to grow in my heart to make our own home a place of safety, refuge, and welcome to any who come. But a single candle burning in the window reminds me of its original meaning: that hospitality is available to any in need or without shelter. This is costly hospitality.

The High Cost of Hospitality

Mike and Terri know about the cost of opening their home. As a teacher, Terri heard about a family living in a cramped trailer whose children were constantly truant. Mike, a pastor, visited the family several times, returning home with a leaden heart after each call to the squalid trailer. Together Mike and Terri prayed about loving their neighbors as themselves. When they learned that the children would be placed in foster care unless changes were made, they stepped up to bat. The sofa sleeper became the guest bed for three little bodies. And their home became infested with lice.

Not once. Not twice. Three times they had the children living with them, and three times the lice came to live there as well. Their own four children were infected, including the baby. Do they regret opening their home? "No," they say. "The cross comes at a cost. It's the least we can do to share the love of Jesus Christ with these children. How else will they hear? How else will they believe?"

When her son's friend ran into trouble, Elsa invited the drug-addicted teen to live with them. For months Eddie used the spare room, and Elsa demonstrated God's love to him, a love that welcomes the alien and the stranger. Today Eddie is growing spiritually and is seeking to lead his children in godly paths.

Jenna and John had known Louise and Frederick since Frederick had come to be their pastor. When Frederick died, Louise was old, ill, crotchety, and living in her car. Jenna and John welcomed her into their home and nursed her through a slow death. Louise's cantankerous ways did not soften. Jenna says it was one of the hardest tasks she ever undertook. Would she do it again? She smiles her gentle, serene smile. "Absolutely."

A faraway friend e-mailed me over the summer. "A teenage girl needs a place to live in the Chicago area while attending a technical school. Do you have any contacts?"

I put off the search, afraid to ask around. The school was too far away for her to commute from our home. Finally, I phoned a friend of a friend who was supposedly "given to hospitality." I had never heard of or met Linda, nor had I any idea what kind of teenager needed housing. After I explained the situation, Linda instantly said, "Yes. We have room. And our home is one mile from the school." I was astounded, the teen's mother ecstatic. I've never met these people, but I do know this: The love of Christ motivated Linda to open her home. The kingdom will never be the same again.

Hospitality is about incarnating, making flesh, the love of God. And when we offer hospitality to others, the Scriptures teach (Matt. 25:31–46), we offer it to Christ, and so the guest, too, incarnates God to us. Such mysterious, miraculous, daring hospitality requires first that work be done to make our own souls hospitable.

Hospitable Souls

The places where I've felt the most welcome are those where the tenant-owners have done extensive soul work, attending to the appointments and furbishings of their inmost being *before* tending to their houses. When we have seen the dirt, dust, and general dishevelment of our own souls, given them to God, and been found spotless after His deep cleaning, we can offer genuine acceptance to others, which is a hallmark of true hospitality. After tending to the state of my heart, I can focus on guests. The attitude comes more easily: I have time for you. You are priceless.

With overnight guests, it helps for me to share my personal schedule. I need soul-space early in the morning, and may say, "Coffee will be ready at five o'clock, and I'll be available anytime after seven." I get up early because I'm not ready for human interaction before straightening out soul and body before God.

This time in silence is valuable because I understand myself better as God reveals my quirks and qualms. In solitude I struggle to answer those prodding, Spirit-prompted questions: *Why do you talk the most, Jane? Why were you jumping up, moving around, changing the subject? There you stole the conversational ball. You're interrupting, finishing sentences again. How about eye contact?* In the throbbing silence God brings perspective and honesty. As I become more self-aware, I also grow in guest-awareness, a key in hospitality.

Guest Awareness

Real hospitality is more than throwing down a floral welcome mat, although visual feasts convey a beautiful message. I'll never forget Karen's table setting: elegant cloth napkins, goldware, and gold-rimmed plates that held a steak, asparagus, and black bean salad on a vibrant bed of greens. Her attention to detail said, "I care." But more important was Karen's attitude. She offered genuine soul-care, guiding our conversation more deeply into eternal matters. Clearly, Karen had prepared more than her home; she'd readied her heart for guests as well.

Most hospitable are those hosts who welcome others, not in spite of their own pain and suffering, but perhaps because of it. Once, after beginning to find healing for a particular past pain, I invited God to bring into my life others in similar places. Over the next several days, no less than ten people appeared, all journeying toward healing in the same area. Kurt Hahn, father of Outward Bound, lived by the philosophy "Your disability is your opportunity." One passage epitomizes the purpose of hospitality:

> Praise be to the . . . Father of compassion and the God of all comfort, who comforts us in all our troubles, so that we can comfort those in any trouble with the comfort we ourselves have received from God. . . . If we are distressed, it is for your comfort and salvation; if we are comforted, it is for your comfort (2 Cor. 1:3–4, 6 NIV).

So after my own soul-dusting, I try to listen. What clues might the Lord reveal about the needs, pain, interests of the other? What previous conversations might provide pick-up notes to further deepen our relationship and lead my guest nearer to the heart of God? Where have I sensed a tender heart, a touchy subject, or tears near the surface? Glimpses of frustration, of gifts flourishing? I listen for questions God might lead me to ask, for stories or weaknesses to share, looking for places to relate in a deep and meaningful way.

Conversational Clues

Even armed with the best of intentions and adequate soul work, it's sometimes difficult to come up with conversational jump-starters. As a dyed-in-the-wool introvert, my natural shyness could easily take over and create stiff barriers between myself and another. Here are some beginning questions you might use. Questions generally move from broad and basic to specific.

- How long have you lived here? Or, What brought you to this area (or church)? (In a highly mobile community, this is usually a safe start for a newcomer or new-to-you friend.)
- How's this past week been for you? (My husband frequently asks this simple starter, and has been led into great ministry opportunities.)

- Tell me about your family. (This lead-in can be risky, but can also develop into deep conversation.)
- What are your special interests, dreams, passions?
- When do you feel the most alive?
- When have you felt the closest to God, the most alive spiritually? (If it's not now, ask them what happened.)

When we've invited God to give us a heart for others and guide us into conversation, we'll find hospitality opportunities every place we look.

Content, Not Context

Hospitality doesn't depend on accommodations and accouterments as much as attitude. Place is much less important than the message conveyed. When Carol answers the phone, her lilting voice smiles into the receiver, and the caller immediately feels welcome. Jolene always sounds like I'm doing her a favor when I ask for help. Every time I phone her office, Kris makes me feel as if she's waited a lifetime for my call.

Recently I arrived ninety minutes early for a flight. The gate area was deserted. One lone employee stood at the counter. A departure sign behind him should have read "On time," but said instead, "Flight canceled. None rescheduled."

Back in the terminal, lines of people and luggage inched toward the ticket counter. After forty-five minutes of exchanging jokes and war stories, smiling felt natural while the harried attendant sweated it out trying to get me home that evening. All departures to Chicago's O'Hare were long gone. The next plane left at 6:40 A.M. I smiled again in reassurance that I didn't blame him for the cancellation. He scribbled out coupons for meals and lodging and booked me on a direct flight for the next sunrise. I looked at the ticket. First class. Without doubt, if I had not been hospitable toward him, I'd have flown coach.

At dawn, I spread out in the extra-wide leather seats, ate with real silverware, and sipped gourmet coffee with real cream from a real cup. Mismatched luggage and jeans may have clued her in to my former coach status, but the hospitable flight attendant treated me like a first-class guest.

I have not always done the same with all who came to the door. I was, in fact, decidedly unfriendly when, early in our marriage and ministry together, I perceived visitors as threats. When two gangly guys from our semiurban neighborhood stopped in, I eyed them suspiciously. My husband took over as host. I left the room. By the time we moved, we'd been robbed several times, and they'd both served jail sentences for other local crimes. They were implicated in, but never convicted of, our robberies. Still, shame burned my soul. I'd had the chance to offer them Christ, to welcome them into my home and heart, and thus into the heart of God, and had refused them admittance.

I don't want to repeat the mistake, and try to remember a monk's words: "We always treat guests as angels—just in case!" Whether in an airport, an office, or on the phone, the hospitable heart conveys the message "You are valuable." One of the most important places to deliver that message is in our homes and to our families.

Family Hospitality

The telephone jangled in the midst of a family disagreement. My strident words to those seated around the dinner table changed immediately to pleasantries when I picked up the receiver. Listening with both ears, I heard in the background, "Daddy, why is Mommy so mean to us and so nice on the phone?"

I am humbled and often humiliated to realize that it's more convenient to have polite, interested voices and attitudes with guests than with my family. It's much easier to relegate loved ones to a "responsibility" slot than to see them as God-given guests in my life, albeit permanent ones. I get so busy meeting their physical needs that I forget about their spiritual, emotional, and friendship needs.

My goal at home is that my family feel welcomed, loved, and precious; that they know "Mom has time." I'm trying to quit work when the bus pulls up or my husband comes home, to hang out in the kitchen and living areas, to simply be present. Eye contact, casual touch, focused attention: such parental tools are practical tools of hospitality as well. I don't always succeed, but if I free myself up to enjoy their company, the chances are good that some family member will plop down on the sofa and open a conversation.

Sometimes, though, it's important to have the same solitude talk with them that we would have with a guest, graciously saying to our beloved family, "I need solitude so I can be wholly present." There are also segments of our lives when we must pull up the welcome mat and close the curtains for a while.

Seasons of Hospitality

One woman in a busy neighborhood made certain that friends of hers and of the children knew the signal: When the garage door is open, you can come, talk, play. When the garage door is shut, we aren't available.

Like the earth around us, we too have seasons for bearing fruit and seasons when we put down roots. Such rooting times may not be seasons for hospitality; times when there simply is not enough of us to go around, or when we may be so emotionally fragile we can't extend ourselves to another. Stress can make us self-protective to the point of crabbiness. With small or special-needs children, our souls can be stretched taut as rubber bands. Times of transition require special attention to the needs of loved ones and deplete our own emotional resources.

These are seasons when we can snuggle up, burrowing deep into the hospitable heart of God, and find rest and healing for our own souls. God will make it clear when we can come up for air and bear fruit again. For the time being, it is important to be aware of and hospitable to our own needs, to shutter the windows for a season, and seek places where we can be nurtured.

Scriptural Role Models

Hospitality began at Creation, when the triune God created an entire world for His guests. Role models in Scripture repeatedly display welcome. One of my favorite examples is of Abraham who upon seeing three strangers outside his tent, ran to meet them, bowed low, and said, "Please let a little water be brought and wash your feet and rest yourselves under the tree; and I will bring a piece of bread, that you may refresh yourselves" (Gen. 18:4–5).

Abraham's offer of water, rest, and refreshing demonstrate for me genuine hospitality. The offer of bread to the strangers becomes poignant when I look at Jesus: turning a few bits of bread into food for thousands; saying, "My food is to do the will of Him who sent me;" saying of himself, "I am the Bread of Life; he who comes to Me shall not hunger" (John 6:35). Christ holds the bread at the last meal with His disciples, breaks it, and says, "This is My body, broken for you." Companion, from the words *cum panis*, literally means "the one who shares bread."

Jesus, who did not withhold even himself but offered himself up for us, bids us, "Come." Share the bread He offers. Fellowship at His banquet table. Join the wedding feast. He will be our host, our companion on the inner journey, our mentor in hospitality. Listen to the invitation: "And the Spirit and bride say, 'Come.' And let the one who hears say, 'Come.' And let the one who is thirsty come; let the one who wishes take the water of life without cost" (Rev. 22:17).

As the welcoming words "Come" sing in your soul, may you find welcome acceptance in the heart of God, and may your life reflect the gracious companionship of Jesus.

Come. Welcome.

Quotes for Contemplation

An open heart and an open home are potential in every Christian, male or female, married or single. Each has a heart the Spirit is seeking to move with the things that move the heart of God. . . . If Christians would open their homes and practice hospitality as defined in Scripture, we could significantly alter the fabric of society. We could play a major role in its spiritual, moral, and emotional redemption.

—KAREN MAINS,
OPEN HEART, OPEN HOME

Oh, Lord, thou art our home,
to whom we fly,
And so hast always been,
from age to age.

—FRANCIS BACON,
AS QUOTED BY C. H. SPURGEON IN
THE TREASURY OF DAVID,
VOL. 2, PART 2

God, our Maker . . . roams the universe, He makes the earth His footstool, He rides upon the oceans, but He chooses to make the regenerate human heart His home. He left Heaven to make His "temple in thy breast" as John Donne said. Jesus abandoned Heaven to live in me; a large price to pay for a ramshackle home. Equally startling, He calls us to make our home in Him. He opens His being to us, flings wide the gates, and invites us into the holy place that we might live there forever.

—JEAN FLEMING,
THE HOMESICK HEART

Yes is the key that opens the door into Christ, our home. He stands at the door, knocking. I say yes *and undo the latch. Will I make my home with Him?* Yes. *If we are to make our home together, He says, I must remain with Him. Will I?* Yes. *This living arrangement is not a democracy. We will not take a vote when we disagree. He is Lord, after all. He will decide for us.* Yes*—yes upon yes, an uncrafted, voluntary stack of yeses reaching into Heaven. The walls of our life together are built by my yeses mortared by His grace, wisdom, and love. I must be willing to live in the white truth of His Presence. Here I build my home in God, on earth, in intimacy, in union.*

—**JEAN FLEMING,**
THE HOMESICK HEART

Hospitality is not what we have, but what we are.

KAREN MAINS,
OPEN HEART, OPEN HOME

In about the first three years of L'Abri all our wedding presents were wiped out. Our sheets were torn. Holes were burned in our rugs. . . . Drugs came to our place. People vomited in our rooms . . . and in the rest of the chalets of L'Abri.

How many times has this happened to you? All you have to do is open your home and begin. And there is no place in God's world where there are no people who will come and share a home as long as it is a real home. . . .

If you have never done any . . . things of this nature, if you have been married for years and years and had a home (or even a room) and none of this has ever occurred, if you have been quiet especially as our culture is crumbling about us—do you really believe that people are going to hell? And if you really believe that, how can you stand and say, "I have never paid the price to open my living place and do the things that I can do"?

—**FRANCIS A. SCHAEFFER,**
THE CHURCH AT THE END OF THE TWENTIETH CENTURY
AS QUOTED IN OPEN HEART, OPEN HOME

Scriptures for Meditation

How lovely are Thy dwelling places,
O Lord of hosts!

My soul longed and even yearned
for the courts of the Lord;
My heart and my flesh sing for joy
to the living God.
The bird also has found a house,
and the swallow a nest for herself,
where she may lay her young,
Even Thine altars, O Lord of hosts,
My King and my God.
How blessed are those who dwell
in Thy house!
They are ever praising Thee.

—PSALM 84:1–4

It is better to live in a corner of a roof,
Than in a house shared with a contentious woman. . . .
It is better to live in a desert land
than with a contentious and vexing woman.

—PROVERBS 21:9, 19

Better is a dry morsel with quietness,
Than a house full of feasting with strife.

—PROVERBS 17:1 NKJV

Above all, keep fervent in your love for one another, because love covers a multitude of sins. Be hospitable to one another without complaint. As each one has received a special gift, employ it in serving one another, as good stewards of the manifold grace of God. Whoever speaks, let him speak, as it were, the utterances of God; whoever serves, let him do so as by the strength which God supplies; so that in all things God may be glorified through Jesus Christ, to whom belongs the glory and dominion forever and ever. Amen.

—1 PETER 4:8–11

And with many other words he solemnly testified and kept on exhorting them, saying, "Be saved from this perverse generation!" So then, those who had received his word were baptized; and there were added that day about three thousand souls. And they were continually devoting themselves to the apostles' teaching and to fellowship, to the breaking of bread and to prayer. And everyone kept feeling a sense of awe; and many wonders and signs were taking place through the apostles.

—ACTS 2:40–43

"Make your home in me, as I make mine in you.
As a branch cannot bear fruit all by itself,
but must remain part of the vine,
neither can you unless you remain in me.
I am the vine,
you are the branches.
Whoever remains in me, with me in him,
bears plenty of fruit."

—JOHN 15:4–5 JERUSALEM BIBLE

Let the love of the brethren continue. Do not neglect to show hospitality to strangers, for by this some have entertained angels without knowing it. Remember the prisoners, as though in prison with them, and those who are ill-treated, since you yourselves also are in the body.

—HEBREWS 13:1–3

And the Spirit and the bride say, "Come."
And let the one who hears say, "Come."
And let the one who is thirsty come;
let the one who wishes take the water of life
without cost.

—REVELATION 22:17

Other Scriptures for meditation include Luke 4:18–19, Isaiah 58:6–9, and Luke 14:12–14.

Journaling

As you journal, ask the Lord to reveal areas in your life where you might grow in hospitable responses. For instance, how do you deal with interruptions? Do certain Scriptures from above burn in your soul? Take notes as the Lord reveals yourself—and himself—to you.

Prayers of Confession, Praise, Petition

Pouring out the soul stirrings and spirit convictings from the journaling time, give them into the Lord's forgiving, cleansing, capable hands. God is hospitable and will not turn you away. Ask Him to fill your heart with praise, and with humility bring your requests before Him.

Moments for Creation

Each occupant of this world is specifically designed for the environment. Dogs' fur thickens as cold weather creeps closer, trees shed leaves preparing for winter, perennials drop deep roots as an anchor against summer's droughts. While enjoying the outdoors, notice how God created a hospitable home for His creation. What other examples of hospitality do you notice?

Silence

Filling our hearts with Scripture, emptying them through confession, freeing them through forgiveness: As the silence throbs around you, focus on the presence of God, letting the quiet lift you to the Lord, bringing you home.

Questions for Reflection

1. When have you felt most cared for, most nurtured, most welcomed by another? What contributed to that feeling? How does that experience compare with your childhood home?

2. If you're afraid to go into deeper territory with guests, ask yourself why. Of what are you afraid? Intimacy with your guests? That you'll be out of your depth spiritually? That questions will be asked of you that you can't answer, or that you don't want to answer?

3. If God has placed you within a family, ask them: What traits do you value most in a home? In our home? What would you like to see change about *our* home, our dinners, our time together? When do you feel special at home?

4. When have you felt at home in the heart of God? How can you cultivate that sense of at-homeness with God? Is there a time when you invited Christ to make His home in you, and you took up residence in His heart? If not, would you like to fling open the door now?

Hymn of Praise

Softly and Tenderly Jesus Is Calling

Softly and tenderly Jesus is calling,
calling for you and for me;
see, on the portals he's waiting and watching,
watching for you and for me.

Refrain:
Come home, come home, ye who are weary, come home;
earnestly, tenderly, Jesus is calling,
Calling, O sinner, come home!

Why should we tarry when Jesus is pleading,
pleading for you and for me?
Why should we linger and heed not his mercies,
mercies for you and for me.

O for the wonderful love he has promised,
promised for you and for me!
Though we have sinned, he has mercy and pardon,
pardon for you and for me.

—Will Thompson, 1880

Alternate Hymn of Praise

NEAR TO THE HEART OF GOD

There is a place of quiet rest,
near to the heart of God;
a place where sin cannot molest,
near to the heart of God.

Refrain:
O Jesus, blest Redeemer,
sent from the heart of God,
hold us who wait before thee
near to the heart of God.

There is a place of comfort sweet,
near to the heart of God;
a place where we our Savior meet,
near to the heart of God.

There is a place of full release,
near to the heart of God;
a place where all is joy and peace,
near to the heart of God.

—**CLELAND MCAFEE, 1903**

CHAPTER TWELVE

The Great Love Affair

In a world filled with longing for a love that endures, divorce statistics continue to rise as we run like Scarlett O'Hara through the fog. Unlike Scarlett, whose lover had grown tired of waiting for her to find her way to him, we will never be abandoned. This Lover waits and woos us back to himself.

Gone with the Wind broke hearts all over America, as girls and women alike sighed with dreamy love for the romance and passion of the love story of the South. I watched the huge screen, enthralled with Scarlett's delicate beauty and iron will, captivated by her beau, Rhett, and always pulling for their love. How thrilling to be loved so thoroughly! To run through the fog and realize at the end of the fog was the man of your dreams who'd been waiting for years for you to wake up.

The Longing Heart of God

I wanted a lover, and a love, like Rhett Butler, rich and suave and charming, with a smirking grin and a constant love who would always stand by, waiting for that love to be returned. My stomach lurched when Rhett stood at the end of Scarlett's nightmare, only to abandon her. He'd grown tired of waiting, weary of her selfishness, sick of her wandering heart.

The Scriptures burst with a different love story, the greatest love story of all time, the story of a Lover who went to great lengths, repeatedly, to rescue His lover, ultimately giving up everything—even His life—to have her.

This Lover will never cancel a date or show up late or forget. There will be no rejection from this Lover. He will never say, "It's over." He will wait for us when we are late and hold us through our nightmares. When we run through the fog, He will be in the clearing. He will, in fact, run through the fog with us! He longs for us without embarrassment and understands our longing heart.

> God doesn't turn His back on our longings in indifference; His longings, a greater, graver, holier yearning than anything we know, unfurl bird wings in solemn invitation. His longing, unlike ours, emanates from a selfless love, not from any need on His part. God is complete in Himself. . . . In an amazing display of longing, God takes the initiative to make Himself known. He must. He is invisible, infinite, eternal and divine. Humanity can know nothing of Him apart from His gracious Self-revelation. He demonstrates the enormity of His love and longing in the Herculean lengths to which He goes to make Himself known.[1]

No one can ever love me as fully or as completely as God can; accept me, draw out my giftedness, give me the perfect gifts that will delight. No one will ever know me perfectly—my whims, quirks, shameful secrets, dreams of the future, weaknesses, and strengths. While I am trying to earn approval from a loved one by working hard or being thoughtful or giving sacrificially or becoming a doormat at the gateway to the world, God is saying, "Come to me. Lay down your heavy burden. Carry my yoke; it is easy and it is light." His yoke is like a wedding ring. God is the perfect lover, the perfect gentleman, the perfect friend.

Remembering Our First Love

In the early days of courtship, anything was a good reason to be together, and Rich and I reveled in each other's presence. We constantly watched for each other's good qualities, losing no time in affirming a gift we saw or a charming trait. We were quick to overlook a problem, fast to forgive. We took the initiative: a gift that would please, a love note on the steering wheel, a cup of fresh coffee delivered to work. Seeing Rich across the seminary lawn, with pounding heart and a thrill of excitement, I would think, "He is mine! I am his!" His love made my heart sing and satisfied me. I looked no where else for affirmation or appreciation.

So, too, I remember the early days of exploring the all-encompassing love of God found in Christ Jesus. As a college student, almost every conversation centered on the newness of this love, on fresh discoveries of faith. Every word in Scripture seemed to be highlighted by the finger of God. "What do people talk about who don't know the Lord?" I wondered aloud with a friend while we studied in the library. I fell asleep every night with the Bible in my hand and my heart, and woke up every morning longing to reconnect with God.

But time passed. The glow dimmed. And just as in most marriages the romance pales after a time, so it dimmed in my love affair with God, becoming more like a casual friendship with the occasional flash of feelings. Reality set in with the rush of living and the duties of earthly relationships.

In marriage, we had to start thinking about bills and degrees and futures and fitting others into our lives. Pretty soon, marriage meant work—cleaning-the-house, doing-the-laundry sort of work. Maintenance mode quickly tarnishes the wedding silver!

So, too, my relationship with God obligated me. To being involved in the local church. Leading a youth group. Meeting with women one-on-one. And the work resulting from that relationship diverted my focus until the relationship itself felt like work. Much like greeting a spouse at the door with the daily to-do list, the Love Affair compressed itself into a perfunctory, hurried reading of Scripture and a listing of the wants and needs I perceived in the world around me that I wanted God to attend to. Something was missing on my end of this Great Love Affair. My heart.

Putting Your Heart Into It

As I grew up spiritually, I embraced a keynote speaker's message: "Faith is not a feeling." I immediately inferred that feelings had no place in a Christian's life. A friend's more charismatic experiences frightened me, being far from the teaching that feelings were excluded from the life of faith. Still, a part of me envied her experiential, almost tangible relationship with God.

When a lawyer questioned Jesus about the most important commandment, He repeated an Old Testament passage, "You shall love the Lord your God with all your heart, and with all your soul, and with all your mind . . . and your neighbor as yourself" (Matt. 22:37–40). Jesus finished with, "On these two commandments depend the whole Law and the Prophets."

Jesus seemed clear about the issue of feelings: The heart is definitely involved in this love relationship with God. Many of us love God with our mind by studying the Scriptures, or with our strength by serving in the church, but we forget the heart of the matter: This relationship is meant to satisfy the heart as well. And what is the heart if not the seating place of the soul and the emotions? Since we've been given emotions to teach us about ourselves and about God, it makes sense that our emotions enter into our Love Affair with God. Where is love without the heart?

This doesn't mean we live on the razor's edge of ecstasy, as if in constant orgasmic state, or with a perpetual honeymoon high of tingly romantic anticipation. No, real life is full of peaks and valleys, straight roads and winding S-turns. It's the ponds of utter discouragement that contrast and therefore highlight the moments of bright-faced joy.

Understanding, then, that our emotions DO have a place in our love life with God, and remembering our first Love, how do we cultivate that love relationship?

Renewing Our First Love: Elements of a Courtship

Marital experts (not martial) recommend that both troubled and placid marriages can be renewed by "doing the things that they did at first." All the wooing elements of a courtship—the quantity and quality times together, paying attention, the special gifts, and finding new ways to communicate—help to revitalize a marriage. So, too, these elements can renew our love relationship with God.

Quantity and Quality Time. One article on marriage resolutions for the new year suggested planning lots of time together, slotting in both quantity and quality time. This is true, as well, for our Love Affair with God. I try to turn to God more often during the day, inviting Him into my work, my chores, my reading, even as I invite my husband into my everyday life. As I become more aware of God's presence, I feel fuller, closer to Him. This is not necessarily deep time, being lifted off my feet while praying; just everyday time together. But it changes my marriage, and my Marriage.

Paying Attention. One of the easiest temptations in a marriage is to stop paying attention. We get so overwrought with our work and busyness that another's acts of love become blurs. I don't notice how often each week Rich empties the kitchen wastebasket or cleans up after a meal, how nice his biceps are or what a beautiful voice he has. This is true, too, with God. Like ballerinas without brakes we twirl through life, not finding a focal point and missing the signs of our Lover's loving attention.

With Rich, when I stop to notice and thank him for the little acts of love, our relationship is strengthened. And with God, when I take time to simply experience His creation—not analyze the amazing butterfly or dissect the ingredients of a spring day but live wholly in their midst—my heart softens with love for God, the Giver.

Special Gifts. A good lover loves to give gifts, and God is no exception. This Lover delights in special presents. Today I could almost see a wry grin on His face when I finally noticed mine. Watching out the window, I spotted unusual, long-necked birds on the lake. Swans, floating by like royalty. How many? Seven. Seven swans. Seven swans a' swimming. By now I was grinning, humming the "Twelve Days of Christmas" under my breath, dimpling over my Lover's sense of humor. With Christmas only a week away, I relished God's timing even more. Life and love relationships take on a special hue and glow when we notice and appreciate those presents.

Often those special gifts from the Lord are given through a friend, a family member from the body of Christ. How God loves to express His love through His people! One friend, longing for the warm beach after a trying winter, laughed when a box of Florida oranges showed up at her doorstep.

Once when our son Zak was little, he said, "Mom, could we please get Kentucky Fried Chicken for dinner?" And, knowing I didn't have the money, I said, "Uh, well, probably not." Minutes later a member of our congregation called and said, "I'm bringing over supper. What should I pick up?" You guessed it. A bucket of chicken! We've moved since then, but a member from a local church who heard the story each year includes in a Christmas card money for fried chicken. Just another precious reminder that God loves to delight us through His family on earth.

Time and again our Lover initiates actions through others with the hope that we will turn and thank Him. James 1:17 reminds us, "Every good thing bestowed and every perfect gift is from above, coming down from the Father of lights, with whom there is no variation or shifting shadow."

New ways of communicating. Communication is an essential building block in any relationship, and when the old ways of talking to one another no longer work, finding new methods of relating becomes necessary. When my daily time with God felt duty-ridden and ineffective, when I noticed that I did all the talking and no listening, I began to revamp my time with this Lover of my soul. More than anything, I wanted to put my head against His chest and hear His voice reverberate in my ear.

The book *Contemplative Bible Reading: Experiencing God Through Scripture* by Richard Peace opened up a new way of being with God, taking the familiar Word of God and beginning to listen for God's rumbling voice through reading, meditation, and prayer on a passage. And then, with the Scripture running through the soul like oxygen in the blood, simply being in God's presence. The term for this process is *lectio divina* (lex-ee-oh di-vee-nuh) and means "sacred reading."

> For we grow in love of God as we grow in any intimate love relationship—through a continuum of knowing, trusting, desiring, surrendering our defenses and fears, and ultimately our very selves, to the Beloved. That continuum corresponds with the deepening levels of prayer which are encompassed in the process of *lectio* with its four progressive phases, flowing from reflection on the word of scripture to spontaneous prayer and then to a silent presence to God in love."[2]

I wept at the sound of my Lover's voice, hearing Him again, fresh love pouring over me, filling me up. Scripture reading and prayer time became an active, interactive, life-changing conversation. Jeremiah sums up the effect of *lectio*:

> The Lord's lovingkindnesses indeed never cease,
> For His compassions never fail.
> They are new every morning;
> Great is Thy faithfulness.
> "The Lord is my portion," says my soul,
> "Therefore I have hope in Him."
> The Lord is good to those who wait for Him,
> To the person who seeks Him.
> It is good that he waits silently
> For the salvation of the Lord (Lam. 3:22–26).

As we wait silently for the Lord, our excuses dissolve, particularly the one about our own inability to love others.

"But . . . I'm a Lousy Lover!"

God reveals His faithfulness continuously to us, His beloved. He is totally aware of our tendency to stray, to wander off and get caught in brambles and hurt by wild animals like a silly sheep. And yet He loves us still, keeps reaching out for us, initiating love, ready to start over. Again and again.

And unlike humans, who would be tempted to try to *control* an unfaithful or wandering spouse, God woos us back to himself, keeping us at His side not by anger or shame but by love.

His love baffles me because I am so inherently unloving. The only part of me that is loving and worth loving is the part that still retains the image of God. The rest has been tarnished beyond recognition, tainted like poisoned wine.

This love baffles me because I don't deserve any part of it. This is wholly unearned, unmerited love. I cower in shame, hiding because of my sin-riddled soul. I am so far fallen from Eve in the Garden, and yet my Adam, the second Adam, the Bridegroom who is Christ, comes searching for me, calling my name, calling me His bride.

I, who am afraid of rejection, afraid of initiating love for fear of being found inadequate, am sought by the Beloved. This kind of love is so far beyond any love I can offer in return.

And yet it is a love that demands a response, an enfleshing, in our lives and in this world.

Love That Demands a Response

This perfect love isn't meant to replace love on earth ("I have God and therefore don't need other loving relationships"). Rather, it enhances and empowers those relationships. In God-become-man, we have the role model for loving perfectly. The kind of love the Scriptures speak of—everlasting (Jer. 31:3–14), unfailing (Ps. 147:11)—all this love talk is grand but ineffective unless it changes the way we love on earth. Because God's love is active, dynamic, cathartic—it demands a response. God's love is a verb, as we see in the Baby born in squalor who would die the death of a common thief. "This is love," writes John (1 John 4:10 NIV), "not that we loved God, but that he loved us and sent his Son as an atoning sacrifice for our sins."

And my love on earth is a response to that love. John continues (vv. 11,

19), "Dear friends, since God so loved us, we also ought to love one another. . . . We love because he first loved us."

How, then, can I write about the marriage in heaven if my own marriage on earth is a mess? If my friendships are on rocky ground? I can write about it because I go back to my love relationship with God, where I am perfectly, sacrificially, undeservedly loved. Then, even when I am angry or hurt or when a loved one has done nothing to warrant my love, I can return love to them. Not easily, not ecstatically—because faith is different than feelings, and when the feelings aren't here the fact remains that we have a relationship rooted and grounded in God's unfailing, loving presence—but I can go back and, in my bumbling, sinful, incomplete way, try to love again.

When my relationship with God becomes an affair of the heart as well as the mind and the soul, then the work that comes from the relationship, like maintaining my marriage or nurturing my children, becomes a love gift, an offering energized by love itself. Love becomes practical as I reveal that love through my life with others.

Hear, then, the call to love, to the greatest love ever known, ever possible. A love so perfect, it must be from heaven.

We were created for a love that will never die, never fade away, never grow old and meaningless, never abandon us when we're coming out of a fog.

A love that is new every morning.

Quotes for Contemplation

Father in Heaven! You have loved us first, help us never to forget that You are love so that this sure conviction might triumph in our hearts over the seduction of the world, over the inquietude of the soul, over the anxiety for the future, over the fright of the past, over the distress of the moment. But grant also that this conviction might discipline our soul so that our heart might remain faithful and sincere in the love which we bear to all those whom You have commanded us to love as we love ourselves.

You have loved us first, O God, alas! We speak of it in terms of history as if You have only loved us first but a single time, rather then that without ceasing You have loved us first many times and every day and our whole life through. When we wake up in the morning and turn our soul toward you—You are the first—you have loved us first; if I rise at dawn and at the same second turn my soul toward you in prayer, you are there ahead of me. You have loved me first.

—**SØREN KIERKEGAARD (1813–1855)**

To feel his love, to rejoice in the person of the anointed Savior, to survey the promises and feel the power of the Holy Ghost in applying precious truth to the soul, is a joy which worldlings cannot understand, but which true believers are ravished with.

—**CHARLES H. SPURGEON, THE TREASURY OF DAVID, AS QUOTED IN ABIDING IN CHRIST**

"Jesus loves me.*" What would happen if I really believed this? How would I be different? What would happen if I woke up every morning with the thought* I am loved*? What if I moved through my day, ate my lunch, wrote my articles, read the paper, cooked dinner, with the thought* I am loved *always in the front of my mind? How would I respond to my children, greet my neighbors, treat my fellow employees, negotiate with the auto mechanic, if I truly lived with a sense of God's love and delight?*

—**RUTH SENTER, LONGING FOR LOVE**

Our dignity is that we are children of God, capable of communion with God, the object of the love of God—displayed to us on the Cross—and destined for eternal fellowship with God. Our true value is not what we are worth in ourselves, but what we are worth to God, and that worth is bestowed upon us by the utterly gratuitous love of God. All our lives should be ordered and conducted with this dignity in view.

—**WILLIAM TEMPLE, AS QUOTED IN RICHARD FOSTER'S DEVOTIONAL CLASSICS**

What we are speaking about, in essence, is "falling in love." It is the inescapable message of Jesus' life and teaching that the only real self-fulfillment of life is in giving it away, in love. And it is through the intimate knowledge of his life and love, learned experientially in prayer, that we begin to fathom that "love is his meaning."

—**THELMA HALL, TOO DEEP FOR WORDS**

Scriptures for Meditation

Here is my servant, whom I uphold,
my chosen one in whom I delight.

—ISAIAH 42:1 NIV

"I will betroth you to Me forever;
Yes, I will betroth you to Me
in righteousness and in justice,
In lovingkindness and in compassion,
And I will betroth you to Me
in faithfulness,
Then you will know the Lord."

—HOSEA 2:19–20

As a bridegroom rejoices over his bride, so will your God rejoice over you.

—ISAIAH 62:5 NIV

Watch what God does, and then you do it, like children who learn proper behavior from their parents. Mostly what God does is love you. Keep company with him and learn a life of love. Observe how Christ loved us. His love was not cautious but extravagant. He didn't love in order to get something from us but to give everything of himself to us. Love like that.

—EPHESIANS 5:1–2 THE MESSAGE

The Lord's lovingkindnesses indeed never cease,
For His compassions never fail.
They are new every morning;
Great is Thy faithfulness.
"The Lord is my portion," says my soul,
"Therefore I have hope in Him."
The Lord is good to those who wait for Him,
To the person who seeks Him.
It is good that he waits silently
For the salvation of the Lord.

—LAMENTATIONS 3:22–26

"Do not be afraid;
you will not suffer shame.
Do not fear disgrace;
you will not be humiliated.
You will forget the shame
of your youth
and remember no more the reproach
of your widowhood.
For your Maker is your husband—
the Lord Almighty is his name—
the Holy One of Israel is your Redeemer;
he is called the God of all the earth.
The Lord will call you back
as if you were a wife deserted
and distressed in spirit—
a wife who married young,
only to be rejected," says your God.
"With everlasting kindness
I will have compassion on you,"
says the Lord your Redeemer.

—ISAIAH 54:4–6, 8 NIV

The Lord your God is with you,
he is mighty to save.
He will take great delight in you,
he will quiet you with his love,
he will rejoice over you with singing.

—ZEPHANIAH 3:17 NIV

Journaling

As you journal today, pour out your longings for real, abiding, steadfast, unending love. Let your journal become a letter of longing, of love-sickness, for the One who accepts you without condition, the One who will never nullify His Covenant of Love.

Prayers of Confession, Praise, Petition

Gaze into God's face as you would a cherished lover. Let His searching love seek out the dark spots of your soul. It's safe to confess those and be freed by forgiveness. With this Lover, we have nothing to fear. Let this forgiveness transform you, turning your confession into praise and then petition.

Moments for Creation

The outside world pulsates with God's presence, and God's presents, to us. The tree, the stream, the brilliant sunrise—all these remind us of a lover's gift, a love note addressed to us. Today, notice what in nature speaks strongly about God's great love for you.

Silence

Silence is the ultimate gift in paying attention: deep, listening silence, when nothing is more important than being with the Beloved. The miracle of miracles is, God feels this way about us! In silence, lift your heart before God, letting Him fill you with His love. When thoughts interfere, keep turning your soul back to God's presence.

Questions for Reflection

1. When have you experienced the presence of God? The love of God? Are there particular spiritual disciplines or exercises that bring about a sense of His presence? What people bring a sense of God's love into your life?

2. What would you change about your love relationship with God?

3. How have you sensed God's loving you, and allowed that love to change the way you love others on earth? When have you sensed God's love wooing another to Him through you?

4. What longings are raised in thinking about a Great Love Affair with God?

Hymn of Praise

O THE DEEP, DEEP LOVE OF JESUS

O the deep, deep love of Jesus,
Vast, unmeasured, boundless, free;
Rolling as a mighty ocean
In its fullness over me.
Underneath me, all around me,
Is the current of Thy love;
Leading onward, leading homeward,
To my glorious rest above.

O the deep, deep love of Jesus,
Spread His praise from shore to shore;
How He loveth, ever loveth,
Changeth never, nevermore;
How He watches o'er His loved ones,
Died to call them all His own;
How for them He intercedeth,
Watcheth o'er them from the throne.

O the deep, deep love of Jesus,
Love of every love the best;
'Tis an ocean vast of blessing,
'Tis a haven sweet of rest.
O the deep, deep love of Jesus,
'Tis a Heav'n of Heav'ns to me;
And it lifts me up to glory,
For it lifts me up to Thee.

—S. TREVOR FRANCIS,
THOMAS J. WILLIAMS

Bring *Still Waters* Closer to Home

If your church or women's ministries are interested in considering the author as a speaker for a women's conference, retreat, or banquet, please contact:

Jane Rubietta
225 Bluff Avenue
Grayslake, Illinois 60030

Music Companion Resource Also Available!

A key Scripture for each chapter of *Still Waters*, the book, has been selected and given an original, artistic musical rendition on "Still Waters," the album. This new compact disc recording (or cassette) will guide and enrich your spiritual retreat and help you to memorize Scripture.

The Reverend Rich Rubietta and friends have written and recorded twelve captivating and inspiring songs that you and your family will find easy to sing and remember. Rev. Rubietta has a music degree from Northwestern University in Evanston, Illinois, and an M.Div. from Trinity Evangelical Divinity School in Deerfield, Illinois.

"Still Waters," the album, is destined to become a devotional classic!

Available at the address above:

Compact Disc: $14.00
Cassette: $10.00

Postage: $3.00

If you wish to purchase *Still Waters*, the book ($9.99), and the CD or cassette as a package, please include the total amount of items plus $4.00 postage.

Works Cited

The publisher gratefully acknowledges permission to reproduce material from the following sources. While every effort has been made to secure permissions, we may have failed in a few cases to trace or contact the copyright holder. We apologize for any inadvertent oversight or error.

Berg, Jeff. "Uncontrolled Spending." *Decision* Magazine (Nov. 1998), copyright © 1998, by Billy Graham Evangelistic Association. Used by permission. All rights reserved.

Bevere, Lisa. *Out of Control and Loving It*. Altamonte Springs, Fl.: Creation House, 1996.

Boom, Corrie ten. *He Cares, He Comforts*, copyright © 1977, by Corrie ten Boom. Reprinted with permission of Fleming H. Revell, a division of Baker Book House Company.

Breathnach, Sarah Ban. *Simple Abundance: A Daybook of Comfort and Joy*. New York: Warner Books, 1995. Used by permission.

Copeland, Mary Ellen, M.S. *The Depression Workbook: A Guide for Living With Depression and Manic Depression*. Oakland, Calif.: New Harbinger Publications, Inc., 1992.

DeBecker, Gavin. *The Gift of Fear: Survival Signals That Protect Us From Violence*. New York: Little, Brown, and Co., 1997.

Dravecky, Jan. *A Joy I'd Never Known*. Grand Rapids, Mich.: Zondervan Publishing House, 1996.

Fleming, Jean. *The Homesick Heart: Longing for Spiritual Intimacy*. Colorado Springs: NavPress, 1995. Used by permission. 1–800–366–7788.

Foster, Richard, and James Bryan Smith. *Devotional Classics: Selected Readings for Individuals and Groups*. New York: HarperCollins, 1990, 1991, 1993.

Fox, Arnold, M.D. "Depression—The Hidden Epidemic." *Journal of Longevity*, 1998 Vol. 4/No. 1.

Glock, Allison. *Special Report.* (July/Aug. 1993). White Communications. 2:4.

Goldman, Daniel. *Emotional Intelligence: Why It Can Matter More Than I.Q.* New York: Bantam Books, 1995.

Hall, Thelma, r.c. *Too Deep for Words: Rediscovering Lectio Divina.* Mawhah, N.J.: Paulist Press, copyright © 1988 by Cenacle of St. Regis. Used by permission of St. Regis.

Hallowell, Edward M. *Worry: Controlling It and Using It Wisely.* New York: Pantheon Books, 1997.

Hancock, Maxine. *Creative, Confident Children.* Grand Rapids, Mich.: Fleming H. Revell, a division of Baker Book House, 1978, 1985.

Hart, Archibald, M.D. *Dark Clouds, Silver Linings: Depression Can Be a Healing Emotion When You Learn How to Cooperate With It.* Colorado Springs: Focus on the Family Publishing, 1993.

Heald, Cynthia. *Becoming a Woman of Freedom.* Colorado Springs: NavPress, 1992. Used by permission. 1–800–366–7788.

Johnson, Jan. "The Virtue of Surrender." *Virtue* Magazine. (Sept./Oct. 1997).

Lerner, Harriet Goldhor, Ph.D. *The Dance of Anger.* New York: HarperCollins Publishers, 1985.

The Lutheran Book of Worship. Minneapolis, Minn.: Augsburg Fortress Publishers, 1978. Reprinted from *Lutheran Book of Worship*, copyright © 1978, by permission of Augsburg Fortress.

MacDonald, George. *Unspoken Sermons* (Series Three). London: Longmans, Green, and Co., 1981. As quoted in *George MacDonald: Selections From His Greatest Works.* David L. Neuhouser, ed. Wheaton, Ill.: 1990.

Mains, Karen. *Karen, Karen.* Wheaton, Ill.: Tyndale House, 1979. Reprinted with permission.

———. *Open Heart, Open Home.* Wheaton, Ill.: Mainstay Church Resources, 1998. Reprinted with permission.

Nouwen, Henri J.M. *Here and Now: Living in the Spirit.* New York: Crossroad Publishing Company, 1994. Used with permission of The Crossroad Publishing Co.

———. *Out of Solitude.* Notre Dame, Ind.: Ave Maria Press, 1984.

Osborn, Alex. *Your Creative Power: How to Use Imagination.* New York: Charles Scribners' Sons, 1948.

Powell, John. *Happiness Is an Inside Job*. Allen, Tex.: Tabor Publishing, 1989.

Rosellini, Gayle, and Mark Worden. *Of Course You're Angry: A Family Guide to Dealing With the Emotions of Chemical Dependence*. Center City, Minn.: Hazelden Foundation, 1985, 1997.

Schaeffer, Francis A. *The Church at the End of the Twentieth Century*. Downers Grove, Ill.: InterVarsity Press, 1970.

Senter, Ruth. *Longing for Love: A Woman's Conversations With a Compassionate Heavenly Father*. Minneapolis, Minn.: Bethany House Publishers, 1997.

Swenson, Richard A., M.D. *Margin: Restoring Emotional, Physical, Financial, and Time Reserves to Overloaded Lives*. Colorado Springs: NavPress, 1992. Used by permission. 1–800–366–7788.

Thompson, Tracy. *The Beast: A Reckoning with Depression*. New York: G. P. Putnam and Sons, 1995.

Townsend, John, M.D. *Hiding From Love: How to Change the Withdrawal Patterns That Isolate and Imprison You*. Grand Rapids, Mich.: Zondervan Publishing House. Copyright © 1991, 1996 by John Townsend. Used by permission of Zondervan Publishing House.

The Twelve Steps—A Way Out: A Working Guide for Adult Children of Alcoholic and Other Dysfunctional Families. Julian, Calif.: Recovery Publications International, 1987.

Walsh, Sheila. *Honestly*. Grand Rapids, Mich.: Zondervan Publishing House, 1996. Copyright © 1996 by Sheila Walsh. Used by permission of Zondervan Publishing House.

Weems, Ann. *Kneeling in Jerusalem*. Louisville, Ky.: Westminster/John Knox Press, 1992.

Woititz, Janet. *Guidelines for Support Groups: Adult Children of Alcoholics and Others Who Identify*. Pampano Beach, Fl.: Health Communications, 1983.

Young, Pam, and Peggy Jones. *The Sidetracked Sisters' Happiness File*. New York: Warner Books, 1985.

Books to Read When Seeking the Restoration of Still Waters

Ashcroft, Mary Ellen. *Balancing Act: How Women Can Lose Their Roles and Find Their Callings*. Downers Grove, Ill.: InterVarsity Press, 1996.

Buechner, Frederick. *Listening to Your Life*. San Francisco: HarperSanFrancisco, 1992.

Burkett, Larry. *How to Manage Your Money: An In-Depth Bible Study on Personal Finances*. Chicago: Moody Press, 1975.

Campolo, Tony. *The Success Fantasy*. Colorado Springs: Scripture Press Publications, 1984.

Farrel, Pam. *Woman of Influence: Ten Traits of Those Who Want to Make a Difference*. Downers Grove, Ill.: InterVarsity Press, 1996.

Foster, Richard J. *Celebration of Discipline*. New York: HarperCollins, 1978, 1988, 1998.

———. *Prayer: Finding the Heart's True Home*. New York: HarperCollins, 1992.

———. *Streams of Living Water: Celebrating the Great Traditions of Christian Faith*. San Francisco: HarperSanFrancisco, 1998.

Howard, Evan B. *Praying the Scriptures: A Field Guide for Your Spiritual Journey*. Downers Grove, IL: InterVarsity Press, 1999.

Job, Rueben P., and Norman Shawchuck. *A Guide to Prayer for All God's People*. Nashville: Upper Room, 1990.

Johnson, Jan. *Enjoying the Presence of God: Discovering Intimacy With God in the Daily Rhythms of Life*. Colorado Springs: NavPress, 1996.

Kent, Carol. *Tame Your Fears*. Colorado Springs: NavPress, 1994.

Lamott, Anne. *Traveling Mercies: Some Thoughts on Faith*. New York: Pantheon Books, a Division of Random House Publishers, 1999.

Mains, Karen. *Comforting One Another in Life's Sorrows*. Nashville: Thomas Nelson Publishers, 1997.

Merton, Thomas. Edited by Thomas P. McDonnell. *A Thomas Merton Reader*. New York: Doubleday, 1974.

Minerth, Frank, M.D., Paul Meier, M.D., and Don Hawkins, Th.M. *Worry-Free Living*. Nashville, Tenn.: Thomas Nelson Publishers, 1989.

Mulholland, Robert. *Invitation to a Journey*. Downers Grove, Ill.: InterVarsity Press, 1993.

Norris, Kathleen. *Amazing Grace: A Vocabulary of Faith*. New York: Riverhead Books, a Division of Penguin Putnam Inc., 1998.

———. *The Cloister Walk*. New York: Riverhead Books, 1996.

Nouwen, Henri J.M. *The Return of the Prodigal: A Story of Homecoming*. New York: Doubleday, 1992.

———. *The Way of the Heart: Desert Spirituality and Contemporary Ministry*. San Francisco: HarperSanFrancisco, 1981.

Ortberg, John. *The Life You've Always Wanted*. Grand Rapids, Mich.: Zondervan Publishing House, 1997.

———. *Love Beyond Reason: Moving God's Love From Your Head to Your Heart*. Grand Rapids, Mich.: Zondervan Publishing House, 1998.

Peace, Richard. *Spiritual Journaling: Recording Your Journey Toward God*. Colorado Springs: NavPress, 1995.

Rhodes, Tricia McCary. *Contemplating the Cross: A Pilgrimage of Prayer*. Minneapolis, Minn.: Bethany House Publishers, 1998.

Rumford, Douglas J. *Soulshaping*. Wheaton, Ill.: Tyndale House Publishers, 1996.

Whitney, Donald S. *Spiritual Disciplines for the Christian Life*. Colorado Springs: NavPress, 1991.

Willard, Dallas. *The Divine Conspiracy: Rediscovering Our Hidden Life in God*. San Francisco: HarperSanFrancisco, 1998.

———. *The Spirit of the Disciplines: Understanding How God Changes Lives*. San Francisco: HarperSanFrancisco, 1988.

Endnotes

Introduction

1. "Moving from Solitude to Community to Ministry," *Leadership* (Spring 1995): 81.

Chapter 1

1. Clarissa Estes, *Women Who Run With the Wolves* (New York: Ballantine Books, 1992), 6.
2. Ruth Senter, *Longing for Love: A Woman's Conversations with a Compassionate Heavenly Father* (Minneapolis, Minn.: Bethany House Publishers, 1997), 44–46.

Chapter 2

1. Timothy Gower, "The Night I Didn't Sleep," *Readers Digest* (Sept. 1997): 17.
2. Hillary Johnson, *Osler's Web: Inside the Labyrinth of the Chronic Fatigue Syndrome Epidemic* (New York: Crown Publishers, 1996), cover flap.
3. Ibid., 14.
4. Gower, 14; Robert Sullivan, "Discovery: Sleepless in America," *Life* magazine (Feb. 1998): 59.
5. Sullivan, 59.
6. Gower, 20.
7. Sullivan, 64.
8. Gower, 14.

9. Ibid., 17.
10. For more information, or if you suspect your fatigue is due to a physiological problem, call the American Sleep Disorders Association (507–287–6006).
11. George MacDonald, *Unspoken Sermons* (Series Three), (London: Longmans, Green, and Co., 1981), 31, as quoted in *George MacDonald: Selections From His Greatest Works*, David L. Neuhouser, ed. (Wheaton, Ill.: Scripture Press Publications, 1990), 33.

Chapter 3

1. Ruth Senter, *Longing for Love*, 51.
2. Nancy Bearden Henderson, *Chicago Tribune*, 6/19/98, sec. 5, p. 7.
3. Janet G. Woititz, Ed.D., *Guidelines for Support Groups: Adult Children of Alcoholics and Others Who Identify* (Pompano Beach, Fl.: Health Communications, 1983), 11–12.
4. Richard J. Foster, *Prayer: Finding the Heart's True Home* (New York: HarperCollins Publishers, 1992) 19–20.

Chapter 4

1. This chapter is a layperson's experience, a collection of references and research and real-life stories that might enlighten the person who struggles in the occasional darkness of depression. It is not meant to be a psychiatric look at a potentially serious problem. The suggestions that follow are in no way intended to substitute for consulting with your physician.
2. Norman E. Rosenthal, M.D., *Seasons of the Mind: Why You Get the Winter Blues and What You Can Do About It* (New York: Bantam Books, 1989), 17.
3. A psychiatrist, quoted by Pam Kidd in *Daily Guideposts 1998* (Carmel, New York: 1997), 68.
4. Tracy Thompson, *The Beast: A Reckoning With Depression* (New York: G. P. Putnam's Sons, 1995), 280.
5. Arnold Fox, M.D., "Depression—The Hidden Epidemic," *Journal of Longevity* (1998): 4:1, 27–28.
6. Thompson, 10.
7. For examples, see 2 Sam. 6:14–16; Ps. 139:19–22; Ps. 3:3–4; and Ps. 51, respectively.

8. Mary Ellen Copeland, M.S., *The Depression Workbook: A Guide for Living With Depression and Manic Depression* (Oakland, Ca.: New Harbinger Publications, Inc., 1992), 19.
9. Lewis Smedes, *Shame and Grace*, quoted by Sheila Walsh, *Honestly* (Grand Rapids, Mich.: Zondervan Publishing House, 1996), 85.
10. A hospital psychologist, quoted by Sheila Walsh, *Honestly*, 92–93.
11. Thompson, *The Beast*, 56.
12. From the hymn "On Christ the Solid Rock," text by Edward Mote, music by William B. Bradbury.
13. From the hymn "Spirit of God, Descend Upon My Heart" by George Croly, 1867.

Chapter 5

1. As quoted in *Reader's Digest* (July 1998): 49.
2. Maxine Hancock, *Creative, Confident Children* (Old Tappan, N.J.: Fleming H. Revell Co., 1978, 1985), 122.
3. A more thorough discussion of self-esteem in women is offered in *Quiet Places: A Woman's Guide to Personal Retreat* (Minneapolis: Bethany House Publishers, 1997).
4. Alex Osborn, *Your Creative Power: How to Use Imagination* (New York: Charles Scribners' Sons, 1948), 17.
5. Rollo May, *The Courage to Create*, as quoted by Karen Mains in *Open Heart, Open Home* (Wheaton, Ill.: Mainstay Church Resources, 1998), 189.
6. Mains, 189.
7. Ruth Richards, M.D., Ph.D., quoted by Nadia Zonis in "How to Be More Creative," *Ladies Home Journal*, 109 (November 1992): 106.
8. Julia Cameron, *The Artist's Way* (New York: G. P. Putnam's Sons, 1992), 185.

Chapter 6

1. Sheila Walsh, *Honestly*, 78–79.
2. Allison Glock, *Special Report*, White Communications, (July/August 1993): 2:4, 9.
3. Psychologist Dolf Zillmann from the University of Alabama demonstrated this finding, which is described in Daniel Goldman's book

Emotional Intelligence: Why It Can Matter More Than I.Q. (New York: Bantam Books, 1995), 60.
4. Lisa Bevere, *Out of Control and Loving It* (Lake Mary, Fl.: Creation House, 1996), 129.
5. Goldman, *Emotional Intelligence*, 143.

Chapter 7

1. *The Twelve Steps—A Way Out: A Working Guide for Adult Children of Alcoholic & Other Dysfunctional Families* (San Diego, Calif.: Recovery Publications, 1987), 44.
2. Jan Johnson, "The Virtue of Surrender," *Virtue* (Sept./Oct. 1997): 74–75.

Chapter 8

1. Gary Belsky, "Win Your War Against Debt," *Money* (April 1996), 159.
2. Jose Dominguez, *Your Money or Your Life: Transforming Your Relationship With Money and Achieving Financial Independence* (New York: Viking, 1992).

Chapter 9

1. Father John Powell, *Happiness Is an Inside Job* (Allen, Tex.: Tabor Publishing, 1989), 25.
2. Ibid., 7.
3. Pam Young and Peggy Jones, *The Sidetracked Sisters' Happiness File* (New York: Warner Books, 1985), 59.
4. Richard Swenson, *Margin: Restoring Emotional, Physical, Financial, Time Reserves to Overloaded Lives* (Colorado Springs: NavPress, 1995), 161.
5. Henri J. M. Nouwen, *Here and Now: Living in the Spirit* (New York: Crossroad Publishing Co., 1994), 31.
6. For more information, see Don Campbell, *The Mozart Effect* (New York: Avon Books, 1997).

Chapter 10

1. Edward M. Hallowell, M.D., *Worry: Controlling It and Using It Wisely* (New York: Pantheon Books, 1997), xi.

2. Hallowell, *Worry*, 58.
3. See Gavin DeBecker's *The Gift of Fear: Survival Signals That Protect Us From Violence* (New York: Little, Brown & Company, 1997).
4. DeBecker, 293.

Chapter 12

1. Jean Fleming, *The Homesick Heart: Longing for Spiritual Intimacy* (Colorado Springs: NavPress, 1995), 32–33.
2. Thelma Hall, *Too Deep for Words: Rediscovering Lectio Divina* (Mahwah, N.J.: Paulist Press, 1988), 28.

Thank you for selecting a book from
BETHANY HOUSE PUBLISHERS

Bethany House Publishers is a ministry of Bethany Fellowship International, an interdenominational, nonprofit organization committed to spreading the Good News of Jesus Christ around the world through evangelism, church planting, literature distribution, and care for those in need. Missionary training is offered through Bethany College of Missions.

Bethany Fellowship International is a member of the National Association of Evangelicals and subscribes to its statement of faith. If you would like further information, please contact:

Bethany Fellowship International
6820 Auto Club Road
Minneapolis, MN 55438 USA